Misadventures
and My Thoughts on God

Laurin Von Krueger

TEACH Services, Inc.
PUBLISHING
www.TEACHServices.com • (800) 367-1844

Copyright © 2015 TEACH Services, Inc.

ISBN-13: 978-1-4796-0491-3 (Paperback)

ISBN-13: 978-1-4796-0492-0 (ePub)

ISBN-13: 978-1-4796-0493-7 (Mobi)

Library of Congress Control Number: 2015907620

Published by

TEACH Services, Inc.
PUBLISHING
www.TEACHServices.com • (800) 367-1844

Dedication

For Jeff Hickey,
You were there when there was no one else.
I miss you my dear friend.

Acknowledgments

Kris, my beautiful husband, I have never had anyone believe in me and my abilities and support me like you. The love God has shown me through you during the rough and smooth patches made this book possible. When I was at my lowest, God brought you to me, and in essence He used you to rescue me, and I know the visa versa is true. I cannot wait until our faith becomes sight and we stand side by side on the sea of glass and meet our Creator and Redeemer for the first time face to face.

Mom, you always had an intelligent knowledge of God and the Bible and human nature, and you instilled in me the desire to continually strive to be a better, wiser person—and not just better when people were looking, but all the time. You are the biggest inspiration for who I am today. I love you so very much.

Tom, my stand in dad, when everyone, and I mean everyone, gave up on me and my rebelliousness as a teenager, there was only one who saw in me what I could be, and it made me want to live up to your expectations. God sent you to my mom and me to save us. I thank God every day for you.

Grandpa Parnell, you have been an inspiration to me for healthier living, because a healthy body leads to a healthy mind. I want to thank you for the countless hours of walks and debates. You helped me think more deeply about life and the nature and character of God.

Melissa, you and your family have loved me even when you've seen me at my worst. And amazingly, you still love me, even more now then you did before. That's true friendship. Our relationship has shown me another piece of the puzzle of God's character.

Dad, I love you …

Jerry and Jean, you are proof that true Christians do exist. You are an inspiration.

Ty Gibson, just a few days after returning from Kris's and my river adventure trip, I drove to Oregon and attended some of your meetings during a convocation. During those meetings, you taught and reminded me of the beauty of God and that His beauty overshadows my ugliness. Freedom like I've never experienced continues to manifest in my life as I remember this truth every day. Thank you for committing your life to communicating this because this message gave me strength to live this life God has given to me, and it inspired me to write this book.

Introduction

"By His life and His death, Christ has achieved even more than recovery from the ruin wrought through sin. It was Satan's purpose to bring about an eternal separation between God and man; but in Christ we become more closely united to God than if we had never fallen. In taking our nature, the Saviour has bound Himself to humanity by a tie that is never to be broken. Through the eternal ages He is linked with us. 'God so loved the world, that He gave His only-begotten Son.' John 3:16" (Ellen G. White, *The Desire of Ages*, p. 25).

Humans are naturally curious beings, we consciously and subconsciously question the world around us, which determines our interpretations of what we perceive as reality. There are several fundamental philosophical questions every human innately asks to which he/she must find answers;

What is the meaning of life?

Who are we?

Why are we here?

What is the nature of life and reality?

What is the purpose of life for me as an individual?

Many people subconsciously seek the answers to these questions without even knowing they've asked them. And then there are times we are afraid to find the answers to these questions for fear our previously known realities and comforts will be disrupted.

Many of us attempt to find answers by looking to superfluous examples, but even when we reach the pinnacle of our lives whether it is career success or fame and money, we still are left void and unfulfilled, seeking but never finding. We see this often with famous actors and actresses—poor souls such as Kurt Cobain, Michael Jackson, Brittany Murphy, and more recently Phillip Seymour Hoffman and Robin Williams—who "have it all" but lack the fulfillment and self-actualization that they are seeking.

At the end of our lives, it won't be the Maserati, million-dollar home, or public recognition for a talent we possess that will stand out. Instead, it will be the relationships we have made along the way that will stand out as our happiest, most meaningful memories.

The answers to the most pertinent questions we ask ourselves in this life lies in the example of the life, death, and resurrection of the Man about whom twelve men, 2,000 years ago, asked, "Who is this Man that even the wind and seas obey Him?" He has the power to do and control anything and everything, but He voluntarily gave up His supernatural abilities because of His desire to have a relationship with us now and for eternity.

For thousands of years people have sought to get to know this Man. But who is He? To many He is shrouded in mystery because His ways are not our ways. He was and is the most selfless person who ever existed, putting others before Himself. He is the perfect example of love because He is love. He is God's words and thoughts and personality made corporeal to show and prove He holds our best interest before His own, despite the accusations contrary. (Read 1 Corinthians 13 and substitute the word "love" with "God," since God is love. This chapter encapsulates His identity to perfection.) That this could be a reality, that there is a Creator and that He is love is the greatest joy that can fill a human's heart, and it's true. I pray as you read this book you will see that this is reality.

Love is all about relationships. Love cannot exist or be manifest without putting another person before yourself. However, because we get caught up in focusing on ourselves and our desires, instead of focusing on others, we do not understand the awesomeness of Jesus Christ.

To further the confusion, many doctrines and philosophies exist that pollute the idea of the character of God. Of course, if there is anything that contradicts the fact that God is love, then that philosophy is false.

In and of ourselves we are incapable of being selfless, only God is truly selfless. If we recognize that, then we understand that when we place our faith in Jesus His pardoning love and faithfulness to us saves us. "But the righteous person will live because of his faithfulness" (Hab. 2:4, GW).

Elohim (God the Father, the Son, and the Holy Spirit) is the God of relationships. We were made in His image, and we were created to exist in a relationship with Him and others. God said in Genesis, "It is not good for the man to be alone" (Gen. 2:18, GW).

God created us to thrive on an intimate closeness with Himself. If Jesus is not our center, true peace and unwavering happiness will be impossible to experience. People who don't understand this often search for happiness and escape in unhealthy activities and addictions. But once the true peace of God that passes all understanding is experienced all else will fade away.

The purpose of this book is to showcase the true beauty and splendor of God's character and how much He desires to have a relationship with us.

Antonio Porchia, an Italian poet born in 1885, wrote, "We become aware of the void as we fill it." Most people don't know what will truly bring them happiness, but those who seek a relationship with God and who begin to love others as God loves become increasingly aware of the void they have had all along, and they find ultimate fulfillment in their lives. The pursuit of riches, fame, promiscuity, and accolades is ultimately meaningless and akin to chasing after the wind as wise King Solomon wrote in Ecclesiastes.

I pray that as you read this book you will learn of the true character of our Creator and that as you move through this life that you will see with clarity the deceptions set before you and be able to distinguish the truth.

"All creation is eagerly waiting …" (Rom. 8:19).

Table of Contents

Chapter 1

Well, I Do Love a Good Adventure

Blue. My favorite color.

It's foolish, I know, but my love for the color blue may be the reason I hastily packed all I owned and moved 1,162.9 miles away. But more on that later …

Blue is simply a visible wavelength of electromagnetic radiation. In fact, its wavelength of about 475 nanometers is short when compared to most other visible color wavelengths, but because of this, it is scattered more efficiently by the molecules in our atmosphere, which causes our sky to appear blue. Despite this drab but interesting scientific description of the color blue, just reading the word can induce feelings of serenity. According to Wikipedia, blue is associated with confidence, harmony, and faithfulness. Perhaps these positive associations are why blue is most people's favorite color.

The color blue curiously holds a special meaning with God—His throne is made of blue sapphire: "Under his feet was something like a pavement made of lapis lazuli [sapphire], as bright blue as the sky" (Exod. 24:10, NIV). It is also written in the traditional teachings of Judaism in the *Talmud* and insinuated in Exodus 24:12 in the original Hebrew that the tablets of stone the ten commandments were written on were also of blue sapphire cut and made from the very throne of God by God and written with His finger. God told Moses to remember His commandments by wearing blue tassels on the borders of their clothing. The commandments of God represent His character of love, so when I see blue, it reminds me that God is love.

We were created in God's image, male and female, with the ability to procreate to show what words cannot explain, that God is love. It's interesting then, but not a coincidence, that God created for us a "blue planet." From space, the earth looks blue, and from the earth looking into the heavens, the sky appears blue.

Beauty Calls

The heat from the red sandstone where I lay emanated through my sore muscles from a long, hot day of hiking in the fiery furnace in Arches National Park. A cool breeze blew off the water of the Colorado River, which smells sweet, and the sound of the water welcomed me home. But these senses fade as the bluest blue I've ever seen consumes me. The color blue is said to calm the soul, and at that point of my life, it needed calming. There is no truer, bluer sky in the world than can be seen in parts of the Southwest, especially in the parks of Southern Utah. If you lie flat and stare into the sky, you feel as though you're enveloped in, and looking through, an enormous blue sapphire. The contrasting red sandstone and lack of air pollution must be the reason for this rare gift.

The first time I visited Moab, Utah, I arrived at night and had no idea the beauty that surrounded me while I slept. When I awoke and walked outside, I was speechless. The magnificent beauty of the deep red towering cliffs, the contrasting blue sky, and the simplicity of the desert made the inmost part of me feel like I had finally arrived home—it was and still is almost like I can more clearly hear and understand God's voice in that part of the country.

Inexplicably drawn to the area, I moved on a prayer and a whim just a few months later from Everett, Washington. Unfortunately, after living there only a few years, I had to move away because of a career opportunity, and I have been trying to move back there ever since. There hasn't been a day since I've moved from the southwest that I haven't experienced withdrawals. The deep blue sky and that distinct smell of the desert air after it rains visits me in my dreams. I try to take vacations back there whenever I possibly can.

My love of Utah led Kris and I to celebrate our honeymoon there. For two weeks we planned to live high on the adventure we both crave, but, little did I know, I was in for a bit more than I had bargained for. Considering myself an adventurous girl, I thought I was ready, willing, and able to take on any daring opportunities put before me. I quickly discovered, however, that when compared to my husband, who is a naval carrier aviator, I am a wimp. He flies jets and lands them on a carrier at night, which no other country in the world will do because it's too dangerous. His threshold for pretty much anything, especially what is considered dangerous, is so high it cannot even be compared to mine. So when I mentioned it had been a dream of mine for the last decade and a half to raft Cataract Canyon but never had because everyone in my past was always too scared to do so, the immediate response was, "Well, what are we waiting for! Let's do this!"

Sounds awesome, right? After all, it had been on my bucket list for almost half my lifetime. The problem? The preceding winter had seen a twenty-year high in snowfall, so the river had reached a peak flow of 84,800 cubic feet per second (CFS). When the river peaks above 30,000 CFS, the river becomes a lot trickier to navigate. At 69,000 to about 85,000 CFS, the waves are enormous and come in quick succession from various angles, bouncing back at you from the 2,000-foot canyon walls. A CFS above 85,000 and into the 100,000s causes the rapids to be washed out, which makes the river not as difficult to travel. We literally hit the most dangerous time to raft Cataract Canyon, which is already a dangerous stretch of the Colorado River at normal flow levels.

Just days before our scheduled trip, the park service deemed the canyon too dangerous to raft because a twenty-two-foot J-Rig boat flipped going over the rapid ominously named Little Niagara. This news made Kris all the more determined and beside himself with excitement because he saw it as a once in a lifetime opportunity to raft with the big boys, so he went in search of a guide company who would run the canyon despite the park service's warnings. And wouldn't you know it, there was one lowly company willing to take on this crazy big water.

A Life in Need of Saving

Six years before this moment, I had made the decision to stop seeking

God. I was twenty-six years old and had previously been on fire for God. Since I was a teenager, I had volunteered for every church activity I could because I was in love with God. At fourteen years of age I attended a Christian boarding academy and was baptized. I was ready to devote my life and all my resources to His work. My fervor waxed and waned for over a decade, but by about the eleventh year I really began to lose that magnificent depiction of God I once had. The darkness of life, my own sinful decisions, and the views others held of the character of God had dampened my relationship with Him. I fought temptations for years with success, but I was beginning to become discouraged because I saw no real change in my mind and heart after years of work. In fact, I felt that I was sinking deeper. So I decided I couldn't do it anymore. I knew I could never be the person God wanted me to be, so I stopped pursuing Him.

I couldn't have run further from the life I once lived. I decided to leave Grand Junction, Colorado, and take a management job in Las Vegas and live the life I had always wanted—a life of freedom from the expectation and judgmental eyes of others, including, to a certain degree, God. Why Vegas? Well, opportunity to pursue my career in communications and journalism, check. Sunshine, check. Awesome music and concerts, check. A large city full of people who wouldn't judge me and would accept me, check. A myriad of distractions to keep my focus off my self-loathing, check. Opportunity to make a comfortable income, check. Anything I could possible want, Las Vegas seemed to offer.

I did everything I wanted. I made enough money to pay off my credit cards. I traveled and took lessons and classes on subjects and skills I had always wanted to know and learn. I saw every show I could and met amazing people from all over the world, all the while barely thinking about the life I once lived.

I did and saw enough to learn sin's honeymoon phase was short lived.

The downfall? Despite my efforts to remain immune from the influences of Vegas, I began to recognize that I was becoming desensitized to some of what I once thought indecent. Fortunately, I kept some of my wits about me and did not participate in many of the opportunities that were laid before me, but I did and saw enough to learn sin's honeymoon phase was short lived. People who were living what they thought was the dream in Las Vegas were some of the unhappiest, unhealthiest, and grouchiest people I've known. Obviously living a life without God in the city of sin was certain recipe for disaster, and I realized I was headed down a path I did not want to fully explore lest I tread down the rabbit hole to the point of no return.

After "living it up" I decided that it was time to be on my merry way, so I moved back to Washington State to be with my mom who had been experiencing some serious health issues. I'm not exactly sure what I was looking for in my life. I just felt unfocused and lost, like I was wandering in circles in the desert seeking an oasis, but never finding one. I thought perhaps going back to my roots would give me some drive and focus, but it didn't, and that next year was the worst year of my life. I became severely depressed, which I had never experienced before, and I just wanted to die. My health declined and I became a void person, mentally and physically. Sin's honeymoon phase was certainly over.

The darkness I had watched in others living in Vegas and which I was now feeling made me recognize and miss the light I used to walk in. Although fairly dim as it was, the light was way better than the life I was living at this time. Instead of having an attraction for certain rationalized sins, I began to see sin for what it really was, and I wanted to run as far and fast as I could away from it. Then I found this piece of truth. "The first thing to be learned by all who would become workers together with God is the lesson of self-distrust; then they are prepared to have imparted to them the character of Christ" (Ellen G. White, *The Desire of Ages,* p. 250).

Chances are that you just skimmed over that quote, but read it again, and then read it again. It is the key to every aspect of our relationship with God, which I did not understand during my years of trying to follow Christ. This complex concept is the key to understanding righteousness by faith. Because we are all broken, we are blind, blind to selflessness, blind to wholeness, blind to beauty. Fortunately, God is a God of rebirth, the God of second chances. He rebuilds and makes whole what we and others have broken, and then, through Him, beautiful things are produced. All of this is possible when God resides in our central vision instead of ourselves. He holds the power to life; I do not. I am incapable of anything good without Him.

Where was I to turn? I wasn't happy being a Christian, but I most certainly wasn't happy living a life apart from God. For many months I only had enough energy to sit or lay and think. I absolutely could not listen to music or watch TV because it just made me more depressed. My mind was searching for answers, and all outside stimuli clouded

Where was I to turn? I wasn't happy being a Christian, but I most certainly wasn't happy living a life apart from God.

the connection for the answers from God I so desperately needed. My mind kept contemplating these questions. Who am I? What do I want out of life? What would truly make me happy?

I was mad at God and blamed Him for the results of my stupidity and hard heart. I tried to forget Him, but I knew He was there and I could never run far enough to escape Him. Every plant and animal and person I saw on my long walks and bike rides reminded me that I was His creation, not a product of chance. My computer is infinitely less complex than my brain, yet I know my computer had an intelligent designer, so how can I exist as the result of an improbable set of life-giving circumstances? So I decided to get rid of every theological philosophy I once learned and start with the simple knowledge that I am a creation of God, and if He loved me enough to give me life, I want to know Him.

I became obsessed with reading the Bible and would pray for hours every day. It was the only thing that calmed my chaotic, restless mind, body, and soul—well, that and chai tea lattes from Starbucks. And no, I'm not kidding. The joy that hiking, music, and dance had once brought me I now found absolutely depressing, and I most certainly couldn't focus enough to do freelance writing anymore. Those chai tea lattes, combined with sitting and reading and thinking while being surrounded by other people, made me feel warm and saved my sanity by causing me to briefly and minutely forget my terrible loneliness, even though I would never talk to a single person.

The road has been so hard and incredibly long since then. It has taken years to recover mentally and physically and spiritually from the demons I allowed into my life. But finally, after nights of sleeplessness and hours of walking miles and miles while praying and pleading with God, I slowly began to come back to life and face my true self. When we see just how wretched we are, it is such an undoing realization. Through the Holy Spirit, I slowly realized I had been selling myself short in all aspects of life, especially my relationship with God, and I had been wasting the gift of life He had given me. I finally became aware of the major barrier I had built between God and me—me. I was a selfish, fair-weathered, theoretical Christian.

For most of my relationship with God, I realized fear of punishment was my main motivating factor to do what was right. I wasn't motivated by love. I had no real relationship with Him at all, with the exception of maybe the first few years following my baptism. But my greatest fear of living a life in hell had become a reality. And even though I began to desperately seek God moment after moment, day after day, for years, I received little to no relief from what I was experiencing, but I knew He was my creator, and I realized as Peter did, "Lord, to whom shall we go? thou hast the words of eternal life" (John 6:68, KJV). The continual prayer on my lips became, "You are my God, and I am trusting in You. Please let me know You and truly be Your friend." I also kept hoping and praying God would heal me, but I realized even if He didn't, my most miserable times with God were more joyful and fulfilling than the happiest times without God. Does this cause me to still be a fair-weathered believer? Perhaps.

Here We Go

I was quite hesitant to commit to my possible demise by drowning. Even though I was on the road to restoration, I was still on somewhat of a self-destruct path from the wave of depression I had been riding for the last few years. So there I was, faced with an exhilarating opportunity but scared to death. When we found a rafting company willing to run the river, my husband was excited beyond belief. I, on the other hand, wasn't confident that we were making a wise decision.

The entire trip from Moab through Cataract Canyon to the mouth of

Lake Powell is about 120 miles. The first 100 miles is very slow going because the river barely drops in feet per mile, but the scenery and wildlife and native ruins make it spectacular. The extra hours of time you get from this leisure part of the run is much needed in preparation of the last insane 20 miles of river. At about the 100-mile mark, the red Colorado River combines with the Green River, called the confluence, and things immediately get very real as the river drops sixteen feet per mile.

These class IV rapids come in quick succession, leaving little time to think. Being from the Northwest, I had enjoyed many whitewater rafting trips, but I had never seen waves this enormous (about ten to twenty feet high). It was almost impossible to talk above the noise of the raging river. It was incredible, the most fun I have ever had whitewater rafting, but I knew Little Niagara was getting closer, and I was growing increasingly anxious.

It's normal for passengers in the raft to be nervous of apparent eminent danger, but I've never seen a raft guide be visibly shaken. About 100 yards from Big Drop 2, where Little Niagara roared, our raft guide, Joe, directed our boat to the side of the river and proceeded to hike to a vantage point to study what many consider to be the crux of the Colorado River. Against my husband's wishes, I got out of the boat to follow Joe to the top of the rock ledge. I wanted to know what I was in for. Even from a high vantage point, the water looked enormous and impossible to navigate. Little Niagara sits on the right side of the channel and is a giant hole about the size of a house, and the hydraulics it creates are practically inescapable if you enter it. There is a ledge wave from the left shore and a lateral wave generated by Little Niagara. Where they meet is the window of "safest" passage, which according to Joe and the other raft guide, Pete, was a wall of water about 40 feet high. Our J-Rig was twenty-two feet long and the height of the wave was a little less than twice our boat length.

Our two "fearless" leaders, Joe and Pete, were speechless and in wonder as we sat and studied the water for more than forty-five minutes. The fear of God was settling in. I was so scared that I asked if I could walk around this succession of rapids, but the canyon walls were too steep and more danger-ous than the river route. The rest of the passengers were now beginning to question their own sanity in choosing such a venture, no doubt due to the very apparent distressed attitudes of the two men who were about to hold our lives in their hands.

I learned two things in this moment. Uncontrollable knocking of the knees and chattering of the teeth like you see made fun of in cartoons is very real when you are scared. Who would have thought? But joking aside, most honestly, I realized I wanted to live and not die. My whole life I thought I had so much time to become the person I was born to be, so much time to reach the pinnacle of who God created me to be, and now I was faced with the potential of a failed and wasted life that could end in a moment. The thought of this was more than I could bear. I had wasted my time on myself.

The next moments brought clarity of focus and answers. I realized I wouldn't have felt like I had wasted my time if I would have just made my life about Jesus and others, but instead I had been a "me-monster." Contrary to popular belief, we were created to share and give. It's about relationships and selflessness—that is the key to reaching our full potential in whatever our career paths or any life path. I had isolated and wrapped myself in a sphere of self-centeredness and not even realized it.

Shaking, we finally made our way down the cliff and back to the boats.

All I could see below me was the plunge pool of Little Niagara. I closed my eyes and waited ...

"OK everyone, wedge your feet into the side corner of the boat and secure your hands with the roping along the edge of the rig, and whatever you do, don't let go." As soon as Joe finished his safety brief, we pushed out. We sat in the middle of the river with the engines in reverse, in attempt to align our timing with the waves timing. Too early or too late and the wave would collapse in on us, flipping the boat and depositing us into the belly of Little Niagara. Finally, the crest of the wave collapsed and Joe put the engine in full throttle, hoping by the time we got there, the wave would have reformed and we'd make it over before its next collapsing cycle.

At this moment of anticipation, even my husband was silent. The size and power of the water in this stretch of river could not be comprehended from our cliff vantage point, but it became very real at eye level. Before we could climb the face of the rapid, there was a hole we had to drop into, causing our boat to briefly disappear from the view of the following J-Rig. I am so glad we were in the lead boat. I'd have been infinitely more terrified to see an entire twenty-two-foot boat disappear from sight. The hole popped us onto the face of the rapid. We were halfway to the top when the rapid began to collapse back on us. Nightmare of all nightmares, death by drowning seemed imminent because we were turning sideways toward an inevitable watery grave. All I could see below me was the plunge pool of Little Niagara. I closed my eyes and waited …

Why Today Is the Day of Salvation

Recently, a very close friend of twenty-one years took his own life. I was devastated beyond words, and even now as I write this I am crying as I think about how much I miss him. When I received the news of his death, I couldn't help but feel like I failed him. Surely I could have prayed more, called more, debated about God more (even though that would have been against his wishes), just simply done more. Perhaps everyone feels this way with the reception of news like this. But in wasting my time and life on myself, I missed countless opportunities to be there for others. Neglect is what happens when love is motivated by selfishness, which of course is not love at all.

I became motivated more than ever to really know what love was and who Jesus, the author of love was, because if I could bring this reality to others, maybe I, with the help of the Holy Spirit, could prevent another person from such an end. "Every soul has cost an infinite price, and how terrible is the sin of turning one soul away from Christ, so that for him the Saviour's love and humiliation and agony shall have been in vain" (Ellen G. White, *The Desire of Ages*, p. 438).

To neglect to show and teach others the truth about the exquisiteness of God causes us to be just as guilty as if we were to outright speak evil of God and misrepresent His character directly. The above quote about every soul costing an infinite price deeply impacted me. I realized that when I am selfish and neglect those around me I, in effect, disregard the Savior's gift of love and His ultimate sacrifice. This broke my callused heart.

I believe at the end of this great controversy when Jesus finally returns we will feel exactly as Oskar Schindler did at the end of World War II. At the end of the movie *Schindler's List,* Oskar breaks down in a conversation with his accountant and comments that he wish he had done more. Even though he saved the lives of 1,200 Jews, he realized that he had wasted plenty of money earlier in his life when he had been thinking only of self. As he began to live for others, thinking of their needs, he wished he had done more. I have a feeling we will react the same way. If only we would have not thrown so much time and effort away, wasting it all on ourselves, maybe just one more person would have seen the irresistible love of Jesus Christ and put their hope in Him.

> *Neglect is what happens when love is motivated by selfishness, which of course is not love at all.*

"For he says, 'In the time of my favor I heard you, and in the day of salvation I helped you.' I tell you, now is the time of God's favor, now is the day of salvation" (2 Cor. 6:2, NIV).

Faced with what I thought was the inevitable end of my life, I couldn't help but think of myself as a waste. I determined that if I lived through this I could no longer in good conscience be selfish with my gift of time. If I can help just one person know the truth about Christ, then I have served a purpose.

Alleluia!

Faced with my mortality, I saw the value of my life through the eyes of Jesus and the value of every other person because of the infinite price paid by our Friend. After I closed my eyes, time seemed suspended and I prayed …

The next moments were nothing short of a miracle. Before the wave completely collapsed in on itself, it reformed, allowing us to right our boat and climb to the crest of the wave, which so nicely and almost instantaneously, dropped us forty feet off the backside of itself. After I wiped the grimy Colorado River water from my eyes, I opened them to see clearly, with new eyes, blue sky. There was no longer a wall of water in front of us; it now was behind us … we were alive! Although the forty-foot fall off the back side of the wave did cause several cuts, bumps, and bruises and possibly one broken bone, Kris and I seemed to be unscathed, just a bit sore from clenching the ropes for dear life. The sky would never again appear as splendidly blue as it did that day God saved us from the pit of Little Niagara. With David, I proclaimed, "He drew me up from the pit of destruction, out of the miry bog, and set my feet upon a rock, making my steps secure" (Ps, 40:2, ESV).

It is because of His faithfulness, not my faith in Him, that I was created and saved to write this humble story of folly. So I will attempt to tell His story, that you may see the true beauty and identity of God.

Chapter 2

At the White House—the Gospel in a Smile

Once upon a time when airports were fun and welcoming and freedom over safety reigned (I'm talking pre 9/11 here), I decided to take a trip around the United States. One day I found myself in Washington, D.C., on a White House tour.

I was tired and exhausted from my travels and was a grumpus that morning. I barely made it to the tour on time, in fact Jonathan and I were the last two people to arrive at the White House for the tour—the doors were shut behind us, and no one else was allowed in. We were immediately left behind by the main group, but we didn't care because we were enjoying reading and looking at the history of our great country.

Even though I was a grumpus, I quickly ditched my frown and decided to smile. I wasn't really feeling it at the time, but I wore it anyway. Because we were rolling solo and had completely lost our group, we soon noticed two men following us. They appeared to be secret service agents. I didn't know if I should or could talk to them, but being the social butterfly I was, I locked eyes with one of the men and smiled at him. His demeanor quickly went from closed to open. He began to chat with me, and soon his partner joined in. Jonathan and I spent the entire tour with the two men, gleaning extra insights and fun facts. To top the experience off, the two men allowed us to play with Buddy, Bill Clinton's chocolate Labrador retriever.

This wound up being one of the most memorable days of my life, all because of an extended smile. It is amazing how hard hearts will melt by a simple act of friendly engagement. The gospel story is told through these simple friendly engaging exchanges over one's lifetime. Any action that reflects the character of Jesus, whether it is a simple act or a monumental act, tells part of His story and provides a glimpse into the true character of God. Throughout one's lifetime these little puzzle pieces lead to the bigger picture, the revealing of the heart of God. Even the decision to smile can change a life and a future.

The Gospel

How can we put into words what we have not seen and can barely imagine? Even with divine inspiration it is difficult, almost impossible, because words exist to describe what has already been imagined, seen, and heard. Despite the clumsiness of words, I will attempt to tell the story.

It ends as it began … in perfect love. The pages in between describe the epic, extraordinary love story of all stories. No book or Hollywood movie could possibly compete. It contains all the story elements a number one box office movie has, but on steroids—the brilliant super hero, the dastardly villain, the betrayal, the tragedy, the intrigue, the darkness, the adventure and romance, the crafty battle of wits between good and evil. It's a story of high stakes with everything on the line, the major players have gone all in, but most of all it contains the answers to every question.

Unfortunately, to many people this compelling love story has become cliché. Its relevance to current life has been lost in translation and undermined. Sadly, the greatest tragedy is that the hero has been made to look like the dastardly villain.

The Essence of God

Before the beginning, in eternity past, before Elohim (the Hebrew name for God, which is sometimes used in a plural sense, alluding to the Godhead—God the Father, God the Son, and God the Holy Spirit) created all that is (angels, the universe, humans, and everything else), the Godhead existed by themselves, living in perfect love or oneness, each always denying themselves and focusing on the other. Because God is love (1 John 4:8), it makes sense that God, who is three, functions as one unit. The Bible does not use the word Trinity, but the three persons making up the Godhead are alluded to in the Old Testament through the use of plural pronouns such as us and our (Gen. 1:26; Isa. 6:8) and are directly expressed in the New Testament.

Love is a theory when alone and is proven when with another.

Love cannot be acted out unless there is someone else to love more than yourself. Love is a theory when alone and is proven when with another. More than one must exist together for love to truly be love.

The Creativity of I Am

At some unknown point in eternity past, God decided to create. Perhaps He decided to do so because God loves to love, and the more there is to love, the more love grows and exists because love cannot be contained. Just as a painter is driven to paint and a pianist longs to make music, God, the supreme artist, scientist, and author, was compelled to say "let there be" and there was. Thus began the existence of time and created beings.

"The Son is the image of the invisible God, the firstborn over all creation. For in him all things were created: things in heaven and on earth, visible and invisible, whether thrones or powers or rulers or authorities; all things have been created through him and for him" (Col. 1:15, 16, NIV).

Hebrews 11:3 says, "Through faith we understand that the worlds were framed by the word of God" (KJV).

We are told in Job 38:7 that the angels shouted for joy when YHVH (the pre-incarnate Jesus) created the earth and the human race, so angels obviously were created before humanity and they watched as God created our world and us. What an amazing sight to behold, to be an audience to God's creative power!

Each of God's creation is astounding, but unlike the angels or animals, human beings were made in God's image. Genesis 1:27 says, "God created human beings in his own image. In the image of God he created them; male and female he created them" (NLT). This verse tells us that both genders as a unit were made in the image of God, which is a living example of the mystery of love and two becoming one. The marriage relationship is also very symbolic of our relationship with God and the parallel is referred to often throughout the Bible. Verse 28 tells us that "God blessed them and said, 'Be fruitful and multiply. Fill the earth and govern it. Reign over the fish in the sea, the birds in the sky, and all the animals that scurry along the ground.'"

So we were made in pairs in the image of God as an example of love to demonstrate to angels and other possible created beings who weren't created as pairs what words cannot describe about the character of God. We were given the ability to procreate (two become three, but are one unit, similar in concept to the Godhead). We are also made in His image because we were given dominion over the animals and earth. We were created with a freewill to enjoy life and God's creation on this earth as we pleased.

"For we are God's masterpiece" (Eph. 2:10, NLT)—we are YHVH's supreme achievement in creation. A lot can be gleaned about an artist's personality and inner thoughts by beholding her artwork. We are to be a living example of God's love.

The Only Non-procreated Ones

Adam and Eve enjoyed constant communion with the Creator and the angels. They and the animals and plants were perfection. There was no flu or colds or diseases, no muscle aches or pain or weakness or tiredness, no sadness or depression, and no death. Any rose Adam picked for Eve never wilted or died. There were no dreary days of rain, for the weather and temperature was continually perfect. The animals had no need to fear Adam and Eve, and they had no need to fear any animal. There was no such thing as predator and prey because humans were fruitarians and animals were vegetarians.

"And God said, See, I have given you every plant yielding seed that is on the face of all the land and every tree with seed in its fruit; you shall have them for food. And to all the animals on the earth and to every bird of the air and to everything that creeps on the ground—to everything in which there is the breath of life—I have given every green plant for food. And it was so"

(Gen. 1:29, 30, AMP). Everything existed in harmony with God's character.

The stature and abilities of Adam and Eve are believed to have been astonishing in comparison to our sin-sick, diseased, devolved bodies. (There are several mentions in the Old Testament of people possessing enormous statures.) I'm sure there are many qualities they possessed of beauty and mental acuity that come from being created as a fully functional human being, not having been born an ignorant, helpless sinful creature.

Adam and Eve lived in the Garden of Eden, which means delight or pleasure. Many have a misguided belief that God doesn't want us to experience pleasure, but He created pleasure and created all our senses to enjoy pleasure—not to mention that one of the fruits of the Spirit is joy! Adam and Eve had complete freedom and dominion over the entire planet. They lived in bliss until …

> *Because we were created to love and true love cannot be forced, God gave all of His creation the freedom to not love.*

The Option to Love

Because we were created to love and true love cannot be forced, God gave all of His creation the freedom to *not* love. If my husband was coerced to love me and had no opportunity to reject me, his love for me wouldn't mean anything and wouldn't really be love at all. For Adam and Eve that was the purpose of the tree of the knowledge of good and evil. They enjoyed vast freedom. God simply presented one teeny, tiny restriction and instructed them to not eat the fruit of this one tree.

The angels have the same freedom to love or not love as Adam and Eve were given. Lucifer, who became Satan the accuser, exhibited his freedom of choice when he decided to stop following God's laws because he felt that they were unfair. He was the covering cherub that had access to the holy mountain of God, second only to the Son of God. He presided over the angels and was their leader and representative who communicated with God. He was perfect and beautiful, perhaps even the most beautiful being ever created (see Ezek. 28:12–17; Isa. 14:13, 14).

The Bible tells us that the problem was that Lucifer got too big for his britches and didn't want to be second anymore and point angels to the glory of God. He wanted to be worshiped; he wanted the angels' affection. He whispered deceit into their ears about God's intentions, saying that God's law of love is a law of restrictions, that God does not have the best interest of His creation at heart. He made God out to be a worship lusting tyrant who is only out for number one, but the reality was that God was not guilty of such things. Lucifer was in fact describing himself in his accusations against God. It sounds preposterous right? But Satan is the king of mind manipulation. Possibly the most intelligent of all God's creation, he knew and knows how to tell clever lies that sound like the truth. He was so convincing in heaven that Revelation 12:4 tells us that Lucifer deceived one-third of the angels.

So why didn't God just smite Lucifer then and there at the mere hint of rebellion and false accusation against God's character? It is because an accusation cannot be squelched by the death of the one who began the allegation; in fact, that would perpetuate it. The only way to silence a false idea is to prove it wrong with a better idea or proof of fact. God had to show all of His created beings—the angels, and eventually humans and other possible beings—that the accusations against Him were and are false. He also had to prove that selfishness or sin, which had metastasized in Lucifer and spread to the other angels in heaven and eventually to our planet, was not the way to freedom, instead it was the way to death and every horrible thing. Selfishness, which is exactly what sin is, must and will be completely unmasked before the end of time. That unmasking of sin and revealing of God's true character began to unfold in the gospel story of Jesus.

The same lies Lucifer used to deceive the angels, he used on Adam and Eve. Lucifer, transformed into a serpent and stationed in the tree of the knowledge of good and evil, asked Eve if it was true that God said they couldn't eat of any tree in the garden. Notice that he, in effect, stated that God is so restrictive that they couldn't eat anything. But Eve replies that they can eat of any tree but that one or they will die. To which Satan replies, "You will not surely die."

It is imperative to realize that God didn't say they would die because of His wrath. Instead, they would die as a result of the introduction of sin and the natural consequence of willfully separating themselves from God's love and protection.

Satan, in essence, was saying, "Look at me. I'm sitting in the tree alive and healthy. I have touched the fruit and the tree, and I'm not dead." Through his words, Satan accused God of being a liar. He planted the seed of doubt in Eve's mind that God's word was untrustworthy. Sadly, Eve was fully brainwashed with Satan's last manipulation. He told Eve that God didn't want her to be as wise as Him and that He wanted to keep them beneath Him in wisdom and knowledge. "For God doth know that in the day ye eat thereof, then your eyes shall be opened, and ye shall be as gods, knowing good and evil" (Gen. 3:5, KJV). (This deception has taken on a vast number of forms with amazing success throughout every generation.)

Hook, line, and sinker, Eve bought into Satan's false accusations about God, making the eating of the fruit certain and secondary. Her shift in mindset gave way to the act of sin. Sin was and always is inevitable if our perception of God's character is false. "The woman was convinced. She saw that the tree was beautiful and its fruit looked delicious, and she wanted the wisdom it would give her. So she took some of the fruit and ate it" (Gen. 3:6, NLT). Then Eve took the fruit to Adam, and he ate it too, knowing full well its consequences.

For the first time they experienced guilt, which breeds fear and self-consciousness, and they realized they were naked. When Jesus came into the garden in the cool of the evening to visit them, they hid. Please note, our Creator desired to draw close to them to tell them the good news of His plan of salvation for their mistake. He knew what they had done, and He still loved them and desired to be with them.

It was they who withdrew from Him and hid themselves out of fear, and with this fear grew the innate human false belief that God is a tyrant and is out to punish us because of His wrath. Scripture clearly points to a God who pursues His lost children. He is the good Shepherd, calling and seeking us continually. It is we who stray from Him. "For the Lord your God, He is the One who goes with you. He will not leave you nor forsake you" (Deut. 31:6, NKJV). God doesn't hate the sinner; He hates the sin. But because of Satan and his lies, we struggle with this concept and oftentimes hate the sinner and love the sin or hate the sinner *and* hate the sin. Needless to say, we are all brainwashed and need to relearn truth so we can be set free.

Adam and Eve were the sons of God because they were created and not procreated as the rest of us (Luke 3:38). Thus they also were considered to hold headship and to be representatives of God to their descendants. When they chose to believe Satan and not God, they effectively relinquished this representation to Satan. We know this to be true because, when Satan tempted Jesus, he said, "'I will give you all their authority and splendor; it has been given to me, and I can give it to anyone I want to'" (Luke 4:5, 6, NIV).

YHVH did not waste time in sharing the plan of salvation. He came to the Garden of Eden and announced the promise of a coming Messiah who would take back that right of ambassadorship over the human race. After He addressed Adam and Eve, He turned to Satan and declared, "I will put enmity [hate] between you and the woman, and between your offspring and her Offspring; He [speaking of His future incarnate self being born to a woman] will bruise and tread your head underfoot, and you will lie in wait and bruise His heel" (Gen. 3:15, AMP).

What YHVH is saying here is that Adam and Eve made Satan their friend instead of God, but God put hatred between man and Satan and sin, and through the life of Jesus, we would know and see the beauty of true love and see sin for the horridness it is, thus setting us free. Satan bruised His heel by having his followers crucify Him, for which Satan thought he had won, but Jesus crushed His head by victoriously raising from the dead, destroying the permanency of death and reclaiming earth and the human race to God. Without a doubt, His birth, life, and death proved His unselfish character of love to every created being throughout the universe who was on the fence about whether or not Satan's accusations were true or false.

Our One True Love and Friend

At just the right time in human history, Jesus became a part of the human race—forever binding Himself to us. YHVH, who knew no beginning and always has been, forever united God and man when He, who is fully God, became fully human. Jesus had an intimate relationship with the Holy Spirit and the Father; they had existed as one since before time began. For the first time in eternity, the Godhead would be separated, and Jesus would know what it was like to be alone without the constant companionship of the Father. The God of creation became acquainted with loneliness.

Lucifer claimed that YHVH didn't understand what it was like to be a created being, burdened with the restrictions that a created being must endure, and since YHVH didn't understand, Lucifer claimed that His laws were unfair. The act of Jesus becoming a man was God's answer to Lucifer's accusation. Hebrews 2:14–18 says it best:

Since the children are made of flesh and blood, it's logical that the Savior took on flesh and blood in order to rescue them by his death. By embracing death, taking it into himself, he destroyed the Devil's hold on death and freed all who cower through life, scared to death of death. It's obvious, of course, that he didn't go to all this trouble for angels. It was for people like us, children of Abraham. That's why he had to enter into every detail of human life. Then, when he came before God as high priest to get rid of the people's sins, he would have already experienced it all himself—all the pain, all the testing—and would be able to help where help was needed. (MSG)

To accomplish this incomprehensible act, Jesus laid aside all His powers: omnipresence (all places at once), omnipotence (all powerful), and omniscience (all-knowing). As we just read in the passage from Hebrews, Jesus had to experience life like every other human being. If He had used His divine powers, He wouldn't have fully known what it was to be human, not to mention He wouldn't have been able to truly experience death if He were a divine, immortal being.

We know Jesus set aside His powers because we are told that He grew in wisdom (Luke 2:52). If He was all-knowing, He couldn't have grown in wisdom. He grew in wisdom or knowledge and stature just as any other human child. Jesus said in Matthew 24:36, "However, no one knows the day or hour when these things will happen, not even the angels in heaven or the Son himself. Only the Father knows" (NLT). If Jesus was all-knowing, He would not have said He didn't know the day or the hour of His return. All the miracles Jesus did in His earthly ministry were because of the power of the Father working through Him, for He said, "the Son can do nothing of Himself" (John 5:19, NKJV). The same power working through Jesus also worked through

His disciples and is available to us. "Very truly I tell you, whoever believes in me will do the works I have been doing, and they will do even greater things than these, because I am going to the Father" (John 14:12, NIV).

In addition to the New Testament, the Old Testament prophets also give us some insight into Jesus' life. He lived one of the most difficult lives ever lived. Satan was relentless in his attempts to tempt and torment Jesus throughout His approximate thirty-three years on this earth. In Isaiah we read the following about Jesus:

There was nothing beautiful or majestic about his appearance, nothing to attract us to him. He was despised and rejected—a man of sorrows, acquainted with deepest grief. We turned our backs on him and looked the other way. He was despised, and we did not care. Yet it was our weaknesses he carried; it was our sorrows that weighed him down. And we thought his troubles were a punishment from God, a punishment for his own sins! But he was pierced for our rebellion, crushed for our sins. He was beaten so we could be whole. He was whipped so we could be healed. All of us, like sheep, have strayed away. We have left God's paths to follow our own. Yet the Lord laid on him the sins of us all. He was oppressed and treated harshly, yet he never said a word. He was led like a lamb to the slaughter. And as a sheep is silent before the shearers, he did not open his mouth. Unjustly condemned, he was led away. (Isa. 53:2–8, NLT)

Psalm 69:20, 21 further sheds light on Jesus' sufferings: "Their insults have broken my heart, and I am in despair. If only one person would show some pity; if only one would turn and comfort me. But instead, they give me poison for food; they offer me sour wine for my thirst" (NLT).

Jesus lived a lonely life. He had never been separated from His Father, and most of the people on earth despised and rejected Him. Even His closest inner circle wasn't quite sure of His identity or mission until after His death and resurrection. All but a few abandoned Him when He needed encouragement and love. Psalm 69 says His heart was broken. It kills me to read that because I, like most, have had my heart broken, and I think I'd rather get my knee caps shot out than my heart broken. I've experienced intense physical pain in my life, but a broken heart was almost a fatal blow for me, the worst distress I have experienced in my lifetime.

Jesus lived a perfect life of love, fulfilling the requirements of the law (the first four commandments address our love for God, the last six our love for others). By fulfilling His end of the relationship (or covenant), He simultaneously fulfilled our part of the relationship. To use an analogy we can relate to, it would be sort of like receiving pay for your work, but, upon realizing that it is physically impossible for you to work, your boss steps in and does all your work for you, forty hours a week, fifty-two weeks a year, but still pays you your annual salary—all you have to do to continue receiving a paycheck is not refuse it. Sounds too good to be true, right? Well, this ultimate gift is a reality—it is the good news of Jesus Christ and His saving love for us.

Not only was Jesus' life one of, if not the most, heavily burdened lives ever lived, but His death and moments leading up to His death were incomparable to any human experience. There have been others who have experienced more physical torture and pain than Jesus, but that is not what took His life and what caused such agony. The immeasurable heaviness of the sins of the world and the corresponding separation from God weighed down on every molecule of His personhood. From Adam and Eve to the last people living on earth when Jesus returns a second time, all the depravity of the billions of human beings who have ever lived was placed upon Jesus' shoulders.

Sin results in separation from God, and YHVH, who was physically separated from God, was now mentally and emotionally cut off from Him. "But your iniquities have separated you and your God, and your sins have hidden his face from you, so that he will not hear" (Isa. 59:2, WEB). Jesus felt the horrifying, separating, crushing weight of sin upon His shoulders, and He prayed for release from the plan, "Father, if You are willing, remove this cup from Me; yet not My will, but [always] Yours be done. And there appeared to Him an angel from heaven, strengthening Him in spirit. And being in an agony [of mind], He prayed [all the] more earnestly and intently, and His sweat became like great clots of blood dropping down upon the ground" (Luke 22:42–44, AMP).

Before any hand of torture touched His body, Jesus almost died in the Garden of Gethsemane because of the mental anguish He was under. Even with the worst torture imaginable, we are only capable of feeling and experiencing our own pain in that moment, but Jesus experienced every person's pain and sin who had ever lived or will live. Jesus' stress was so severe He experienced hematidrosis, a rare condition where a person oozes blood from parts of their body. He was about to die literally of a broken heart, but an angel came and revived Him.

Jesus prayed, but there was no reply—God the Father was silent. The connection with His Father had given Him supernatural knowledge about the future and supernatural powers in His ministry, but now Jesus couldn't see beyond the darkness of the cross and the grave. In His fully human state with the sins of the world upon His shoulders, He questioned the success of His mission on earth. At this point He didn't have the assurance that he would rise again because darkness was clouding His mind, but He prayed, "Not my will, but yours Father." Jesus moved forward despite His fear of staying in the grave forever. He made the conscious choice to save us even if it meant eternal death for Him. Jesus' love for us drove Him to give up everything. He would have rather died an eternal death than live eternal life without you and me. "Set me as a seal upon your heart, as a seal upon your arm; For love *is as* strong as death, jealousy *as* cruel as the grave; its flames *are* flames of fire, a most vehement flame. Many waters cannot quench love, nor can the floods drown it" (Song of Sol. 8:6, 7, NKJV).

Then upon the cross, Jesus cried, "My God, my God, why hast thou forsaken me?" (Mark 15:34, KJV). These are the words of someone who believes He is defeated.

The angels stood poised, waiting with shortness of breath, so as not to miss the slightest twinge of a rescue command, but it never came. Finally, the torment of watching Jesus suffer was over. Checkmate, Satan, or so he thought. After resting in the tomb on the Sabbath, Sunday dawned a new and glorious day. How jubilant it had to have been to be the angels who rolled the stone aside at Jesus' tomb and watched Him walk forth. While the angels of the Lord rejoiced with unutterable joy, Satan shook with unutterable fear. Access for him to heaven was now permanently denied, and he knew his time was short. Satan had no more leg to stand on in his accusations against the character of God or claim to man. "Therefore, rejoice, O heavens! And you who live in the heavens, rejoice! But terror will come on the earth and sea, for the devil has come down to you in great anger, knowing that he has little time" (Rev. 12:12, NLT).

The popular Christian belief of the reason God sent Jesus to live on this earth and die for humanity's sins is that God is wrathful and vengeful and a sacrifice was needed to appease Him. In the popular Christian song "In Christ Alone," one of the lines states, "the wrath of God was satisfied." This particular mindset is disturbing because it is very similar to the pagan rituals where a sacrifice was made to pacify the gods. This was not the reason Jesus came, and it was certainly not the reason for the Old Testament sacrificial system. A very insightful verse in the Bible is Hosea 6:6: "I don't want your sacrifices—I want your love; I don't want your offerings—I want you to know me" (TLB). The Old Testament sacrificial system was a promise of the coming of the Lamb of God.

"For our sake He made Christ [virtually] to be sin Who knew no sin, so that in and through Him we might become [endued with, viewed as being in, and examples of] the righteousness of God [what we ought to be, approved and acceptable and in right relationship with Him, by His goodness]" (2 Cor. 5:21, AMP). Jesus became sin, not because God needed to be appeased, but because He was angry with Satan and sin itself and He wanted to prove Satan wrong and show that He is a loving God. "And without controversy great is the mystery of godliness: God was manifest in the flesh, justified in the Spirit, seen of angels, preached unto the Gentiles, believed on in the world, received up into glory" (1 Tim. 3:16, KJV). Paul said Jesus was justified in the spirit. This implies that there was an accusation against Him that He came to disprove, which is the main purpose for Jesus' incarnation.

"We love Him because He first loved us" (1 John 4:19, NKJV). When we see the true character of God, we change our behavior. His pursuing love for us motivates us to change our rebellious behavior. By focusing on Him and His selflessness, we begin to recognize that Satan and his ways lead to despair in this life and death in the next life. By beholding God's healing character and divine plans for us, we begin to draw closer to Him and grow in love with Him. The more we focus on the character of God, the more we become like Him. This is righteousness by faith motivated by love. "For in Christ, neither our most conscientious religion nor disregard of religion amounts to anything. What matters is something far more interior: faith expressed in love" (Gal. 5:6, MSG).

The Man Christ Jesus

"I heard a loud shout from the throne, saying, 'look, God's home is now among his people! He will live with them, and they will be his people. God himself will be with them" (Rev. 21:3, NLT).

God cannot bear the thought of living for eternity without you or anyone else. His will is that all should be saved. Revelation says that in the earth made new Jesus will choose to be with us because He is physically a part of the human race. Jesus became human and will forever be fully God and human. We will be His brothers and sisters and family (John 15:15; Matt. 12:48, 49).

"For a child will be born to us, a son will be given to us; And the government will rest on His shoulders; And His name will be called Wonderful Counselor, Mighty God, Eternal Father, Prince of Peace." Isaiah 9:6 NASB. God *gave* His son to us. He will not take back what He gave. First Timothy 2:5 says, "For, there is one God and one Mediator who can reconcile God and humanity—the man Christ Jesus" (NLT). Jesus did not wear a disposable human costume for thirty-three years. He remains the divine man, Christ Jesus.

Jesus possesses a human body bearing the scars of His sacrifice, even after His resurrection. If He didn't have a human body, there would be no visible or touchable scars in His hands, feet, and side. "Then he said to Thomas, 'Put your finger here, and look at my hands. Put your hand into the wound in my side. Don't be faithless any longer. Believe!'" (John 20:27, NLT). Jesus' scars are real; they can be seen and touched. For eternity they will be a reminder of the ugliness of sin and the beauty of love.

That Jesus did not return to His full former divine existence seems incomprehensible— what a sacrifice for us who completely don't understand what He went through or how deep His love is for us and all His creation. Jesus told His disciples, "It is best for you that I go away, because if I don't, the Advocate [Holy Spirit] won't come. If I do go away, then I will send him to you" (John 16:7, NLT). Therefore,

We will finally be united with the One for whom we've been missing and longing for our entire lives but have never seen.

Jesus has given up His power of omnipresence. Perhaps we are afraid of this thought because we feel we would be undermining the power and awesomeness of God. On the contrary, this proves His inconceivable love, which is ultimate power. Jesus was translated and given a perfect body when He was resurrected from the dead, just as we will be made immortal when Jesus comes a second time.

Why was it better for Jesus to go and for the Holy Spirit to come? The Holy Spirit can be omnipresent, but Jesus cannot because He is forever tied to humanity, a Friend who sticks closer than a brother.

Relationships refined by fire make the purest of love, and I would most certainly say our relationship with God in this life is being refined by fire, so it stands to reason that after the great controversy is finished we will experience a relationship with Jesus exponentially closer than if we had never sinned. We will finally be united with the One for whom we've been missing and longing for our entire lives but have never seen.

But is it our faith in Christ that saves us or His faithfulness? To be continued in the next chapter ...

Chapter 3

Jesus Pursues Even the Youngest Minds

Gently, Grandma rocked me back and forth while I listened to her hum the hymn "The Old Rugged Cross," which was her favorite hymn. I could hear the rain hitting the window next to her rocking chair—the rain on the window and the melody of her hum combined to make a most engaging chorus. I can't quite describe in words the tranquility I felt in Grandma's arms. I've lain on pristine, powdery white sand beaches listening to the sound of gentle waves breaking ashore, which is my idea of perfect paradise, but it still doesn't come close to Grandma's touch and the sound of her voice.

"Grandma, do you love me?"

She gave me a huge squeeze, "Why of course I do, sweetheart, so very much." Continuing to hold me in her arms, she sang the last verse of "The Old Rugged Cross."

"Grandma, do you really love me?"

"More than you know. And Jesus even more than I."

"But Grandma, how much do you love me?"

This time she stopped rocking the chair, and as I looked into her eyes, I noticed tears starting to form. "Sweetheart, you're reminding me of when Jesus asked Peter three times if he loved Him."

"Who's Peter?" I asked.

Grandma told me the story of Simon, the fisherman, who Jesus called Peter, the rock. She explained that when Jesus needed Peter the most, when

He desperately needed someone to identify with Him and connect with Him, during His loneliest hours, he denied knowing Him and abandoned Jesus.

So Christ, appearing after His resurrection on the shore of Galilee, nostalgically offers some fishing advice as He did three years prior when He first said to Peter, "Come, follow Me." As they are relaxing by the fire, Jesus addresses Peter's denial by asking him three times if he loves Him. Now a humble man, Peter says, "Yes, Lord, I do. You know I do." So Jesus tells Peter to feed His lambs and take care of His sheep. And as this beautiful reconciliation takes place, Jesus brings the story full circle by telling Peter to "follow Me," just as He did in their first encounter on the same shore. Because of Peter's remorse and his recognition that he could not lean on his own understanding and strength, he was ready to complete a great work for Jesus.

I was too young to fully understand much of the theology she was telling me, but I was captivated because somehow it was clear in my five-year-old mind that Jesus had a heart that feels and Peter had hurt it.

I hadn't heard anyone speak of Jesus this way. He was always portrayed as being so nonhuman, so unable to relate to us and unreachable, but the Bible is clear that Jesus was very human and experienced, to the same degree and even more, the feelings, emotions, temptations and sadness that we experience. God the Father and the Holy Spirit are also invested and involved in every aspect of our lives. They are not emotionless, impersonal, and absent, residing in some other dimension.

This is the first memory I have of Jesus introducing Himself to me.

God Continues His Pursuit, Fast Forward Seven Years

"Did you know when you look at a star, you are looking back in time?"

"Um … nope, what do you mean?" I thought he was just trying to be silly. It was unlike Matt to be serious or ask thought-provoking questions, but then again what thirteen-year-old boy really is serious, especially around his peers? Maybe the sweet fragrance of the cottonwood trees in the warm summer night air was to blame for the peculiar mood as we walked. Those nights in Washington State are rare and can cause one's mind to wonder and imagine. But still, a walk back home after a night of sneaking out of the house to meet up with other thrill-seeking friends was hardly the ripe environment for such a conversation.

"Our closest stars are Alpha and Proxima Centauri, which are about 4.3 light years away. Which means it takes 4.3 years for their light to reach us, so we are seeing those stars as they were 4.3 years in the past. And most stars and galaxies are further out, some even hundreds and thousands and millions of light years away. We get to see parts of our universe as it existed thousands, maybe millions of years in the past."

"Wow … well, do you think the universe has existed for such an unimaginable amount of time?"

Shrugging his shoulders, he turned down his driveway, "I don't know … yet."

A surge of adrenaline came over me as I walked down my driveway and looked at the sliding glass door. It was my common practice to take walks alone in the summer after my parents were asleep. Even if I wasn't up to mischief, I always got that tinge of fear when it was time to sneak back in. This time as I opened the slider and stealthily crept down the hall to my room, I heard the TV on in my parents room and knew …

Somehow as I lay in bed, in spite of the overwhelming fear of the wrath that was to come, I managed to fall asleep, but it was a short-lived rest.

"LAURIN! LAURIN!"

Jumping out of bed, I looked up, and there was what I feared most in this world—my mother's hurt and disappointed face. I would have rather faced rejection and judgment from a gymnasium full of prima donna female cheerleading peers as they hurled insults at me while in my birthday suit. I expected yelling and anger and never-ending punishment, but instead I got a disappointed, terribly sad look that seemed to last an eternity, followed by a rhetorical question: "You don't even feel the least bit sorry? Do you?" I sat there sleepy eyed, in shock, and glossed over, completely at a loss for words. "You need to get on your knees and pray to *want* to be sorry." With that last statement, she turned and left me alone in my room.

Time seemed to stop, and Mom's last words, that last sentence, maybe seemingly insignificant to many, made me feel as though I had been knocked on the side of my head. Those words, spoken through Mom by the Holy Spirit, pierced my heart sharper than any two-edged sword. Intense emotion and tears replaced blankness, followed by me kneeling and taking to heart her advice to ask to *want* to be sorry because I truly was not sorry. I had only cared about not getting caught.

Pistis Christou

If we closely reflect on our past, we can recognize times in our lives and childhood when Jesus has been pursuing, knocking, and begging to introduce His true self to us. Jesus tells us in Revelation 3:20, "Behold, I stand at the door and knock. If anyone hears my voice and opens the door, then I will come in to him, and will dine with him, and he with me" (WEB). Francis Thompson called Him the "Hound of Heaven." But the gallant Jesus will not force His will on anyone, because it is impossible to coerce someone to love you, instead, He says in Hosea 2:14, "I am going to attract her" (NCV).

> *If we closely reflect on our past, we can recognize times in our lives and childhood when Jesus has been pursuing, knocking, and begging to introduce His true self to us.*

Contrary to Satan's agenda and false claims, God doesn't do anything by force. Satan thought that once he killed Jesus he would win the war. He thought he'd win the war by force because that is his mode of operation, but his perception of God and God's power is drastically misunderstood. Satan thought he was tempting Jesus by shouting through people to prove He was the Messiah by saving Himself from the cross, but in Jesus exists no presence of selfishness. Jesus sought the will of the Father and thought nothing of Himself.

When we recognize God's relentless, faithful, loving pursuit of us, we are attracted to Him. This is where His power lies. If there is anything good that happens in life, it is because of God. Every hug from our loved ones, every smile from a stranger, every overwhelming compulsion to laugh and find the joy in life, the sound of the ocean waves and the song of every bird, the ability to understand and learn new concepts, the beautiful bright pink pedals of a daisy, and the wet, licking kisses we get from a dog—all of these moments are gifts and reminders to every person of how much God loves us and is there and will never leave our sides. We are the ones who push Him out and lock the door behind Him.

Every good gift is from our heavenly Father, but we often credit our own hard work, drive, money, education, or anything else but God. Of course, when everything goes poorly, we immediately blame God, but everything opposite of love and joy is not of God, but of Satan. We would do well to recognize that in every circumstance the "Hound of Heaven" is prompting and teaching and giving wisdom and calling.

"They know the truth about God because he has made it obvious to them. For ever since the world was created, people have seen the earth and sky. Through everything God made, they can clearly see his invisible qualities—his eternal power and divine nature. So they have no excuse for not knowing God. Yes, they knew God, but they wouldn't worship him as God or even give him thanks. And they began to think up foolish ideas of what God was like. As a result, their minds became dark and confused. Claiming to be wise, they instead became utter fools" (Rom. 1:19–22, NLT).

Paul wrote many times about the pursuant Jesus. There has been an ongoing thirty-year debate concerning the meaning of the Greek phrase, *pistis Christou,* which Paul wrote and which translates to "faith Christ." Most Bibles translate this phrase into the objective genitive, which reads, "faith in Christ." But for the last thirty years writers such as Tom Wright and Richard Hays have suggested that *pistis Christou* should be translated into the subjective genitive, which would read "the faithfulness of Christ."

Below are a few examples of Bible texts to compare:

Roman 3:21, 22

Objective genitive –"But now the righteousness of God has been manifested apart from the law, although the Law and the Prophets bear witness to it—*the righteousness of God through faith in Jesus Christ for all who believe*" (ESV).

Subjective genitive –"But now, apart from the Law, God's righteousness is revealed and is attested by the Law and the Prophets—*God's righteousness through the faithfulness of Jesus the Messiah*—for all who believe" (ISV).

Galatians 2:16–20

Objective genitive – "Know that a person is not justified by the works of the law, but by *faith in Jesus Christ. So we, too, have put our faith in Christ Jesus that we may be justified by faith in Christ* and not by the works of the law, because by the works of the law no one will be justified. But if, in seeking to be justified in Christ, we Jews find ourselves also among the sinners, doesn't that mean that Christ promotes sin? Absolutely not! If I rebuild what I destroyed, then I really would be a lawbreaker. For through the law I died to the law so that I might live for God. I have been crucified with Christ and I no longer live, but Christ lives in me. The life I now live in the body, *I live by faith in the Son of God,* who loved me and gave himself for me" (NIV).

Subjective genitive – "Yet we know that a person is not justified by doing what the Law requires, but rather by the *faithfulness of Jesus the Messiah. We, too, have believed in the Messiah Jesus so that we might be justified by the faithfulness of the Messiah* and not by doing what the Law requires, for no human being will be justified by doing what the Law requires. Now if we, while trying to be justified by the Messiah, have been found to be sinners, does that mean that the Messiah is serving the interests of sin? Of course not! For if I rebuild something that I tore down, I demonstrate that I am a wrongdoer. For through the Law I died to the Law so that I might live for God. I have been crucified with the Messiah. I no longer live, but the Messiah lives in me, and the life that I am now living in this body *I live by the faithfulness of the Son of God, who loved me and gave himself for me*" (ISV).

Philippians 3:9

Objective genitive –"I no longer count on my own righteousness through obeying the law; rather, *I become righteous through faith in Christ*" (NLT).

Subjective genitive –"Not having a righteousness of my own that comes from the Law, *but one that comes through the faithfulness of the Messiah*, the righteousness that comes from God and that depends on faith" (ISV).

Both faith in Christ and the faithfulness of Christ are sublime and, in a sense, correct translations. And both are important in having a relationship with Jesus, just as it takes both person's faith and faithfulness in a marriage to be successful. But is one more correct? Yes, there is a more correct interpretation. It is the faithfulness of Jesus Christ our Messiah. If it wasn't for Him, we would not even have the opportunity to have faith in Him because we would not even be able to breath at this very moment; we would simply not exist. His faithfulness to the Father and us is what has afforded us every opportunity for love, life, eternal life, hope, freedom, and every other wonderful thing that exists now and that will exist in eternity future.

The biggest issue with translating *pistis Christou* to "faith in Christ" is it insinuates that our salvation is in our own hands. It is a salvation by works mindset. It is saying that because of our faith in Him we are saved, but that is not true. It is because of His sacrifice, His faithful obedience to God, that we are saved. We are saved by the grace of Jesus and the Father. "He saved us, not because of the righteous things we had done [because we have done absolutely nothing righteous], but because of his mercy. He washed away our sins, giving us a new birth and new life through the Holy Spirit" (Titus 3:5, NLT).

"No one is righteous—not even one. No one is truly wise; no one is seeking God. All have turned away; all have become useless. No one does good, not a single one" (Rom. 3:10–12, NLT). No one can be "good enough" to be saved, but there was one human who was, and that was Christ Jesus. Our duty is to accept His free gift—that's all there is to it. And then, if you love Him and seek Him, the Holy Spirit will begin to live in your heart. God knew it was impossible for a human to be righteous and live in accordance to His law of love, so He knew He had to do it Himself, fulfilling the covenant from our end and His end by becoming human. Now that's amazing grace.

Ezekiel 11:19 says, "I will give them an undivided heart and put a new spirit in them; I will remove from them their heart of stone and give them a heart of flesh" (NIV).

When the Holy Spirit lives in our heart and mind, our thoughts and desires will become like Jesus' and, without even trying, we will begin to keep His law of love. It's an automatic response, not something we work at. It's a result of answering Jesus' knock and opening the door and inviting Him in. As we read above, we do not seek Him; He seeks us, He pursues us, He is faithful to us. Once we invite Jesus in, His beauty becomes our beauty. "Whatever is honorable, whatever is just, whatever is pure, whatever is lovely, whatever is commendable, if there is any excellence, if there is anything worthy of praise, think about these things" (Phil. 4:8, ESV).

And if we are not at a point where we want to beautify our minds and lives, if we don't want to quite smoking, or clubbing, or drinking, or being promiscuous, or any other vice that may have ahold of our heart and life, then we can ask for the desire to want to trash the darkness out of our lives and invite Jesus in. He says to test Him and to come reason with Him. If we keep inviting and asking, miracles will happen, love will happen, and the fruits of the Holy Spirit will happen—"But the Holy Spirit produces this kind of fruit in our lives: love, joy, peace, patience, kindness, goodness, faithfulness, gentleness, and self-control. There is no law against these things!" (Gal. 5:22, 23, NLT).

Our faith in Jesus grows as we become increasingly aware of His faithfulness to us.

Our faith in Jesus grows as we become increasingly aware of His faithfulness to us. *Pistis Christou*—the faithfulness of Jesus Christ our Messiah.

Chapter 4

Light From "One" Direction

In the movie *City Slickers* Mitch Robbins is a witty and endearing character from New York City who's been lured by his best friends to embark on a two-week cattle drive "vacation" in the southwest. Hilarity ensues as his journey creates a mental paradigm shift, causing him to more clearly reflect on his midlife crisis and his failing marriage.

The ranch's trail boss, Curly, who has little use for words and who has quite an allure, yet demands a frightening respect only a hardened, leatherlike cowboy can, becomes a contributing catalyst in Mitch's journey when he tells him that the secret to life is finding and sticking to "one thing." When Mitch asks him what the one thing is, Curly tells him that he has to figure that out for himself.

It's profound advice with layers of meaning perhaps beyond what the writers of this comedy intended. In fact, I don't think a theologian could have been more poignant—although Jesus was.

The Never-ending Story Wherever the Gospel Is Preached

"There is only one thing worth being concerned about. Mary has discovered it and it will not be taken away from her" (Luke 10:42, NLT).

Affectionately she reflected on her life as it had been and as it was now. She was astonished at her renewed vivacity. Grateful for the emancipation the

Teacher had given her, she was moved with compassion to honor Him, and yet now she froze in anticipation and angst. She had just spent a year's wages on a polished white, translucent, hand carved box full of the rare exquisite oil-based perfume of spikenard.

At one time her blossoming life was so exciting that she couldn't wait to rise early in the morning. Nothing was impossible, and when sadness or loneliness came, there was always a joyful hope that lived in her heart that only the presence of the Holy Spirit can deliver.

Her young self viewed the world through dynamic colored lenses of hope in the possibilities of the unknown. She had a vivid imagination and an inspired heart. Nothing was impossible …

But regrettably she had not chosen wisely. She had a curiosity for what most of the world calls pleasure. Little by little Satan diminished that light in her heart and mind through malignant relationships beginning in lust and ending in infidelity. She was abused by people she desperately wanted to trust. She witnessed the death of loved ones and illness and pain. She wasn't created with the ability to endure such cruelty, especially with a desperate heart for love as big as hers. Most of her sorrow was self-inflicted, but much of it was not. Gradually Satan extinguished all the light and claimed her as his own. She was stuck in the miry pit beyond anyone's reach, a victim of Satan and her own self-destructive addictions and compulsions … until she found the "one thing."

An Introduction to His Faithfulness

Wordless and shaking, she sat in the dirt awaiting her death sentence. She bore the not so discernible scars of a victim of abuse since a young girl. She had been taken advantage of and hence placed her self-worth on who wanted to be in her intimate company. She was now the victim of the Pharisees in yet another conspiracy as they plotted to trap Jesus with His own words.

The Pharisees had just so happened to conveniently catch her in adultery, but the second guilty party in the matter had suspiciously slipped away. In Deuteronomy, Moses said both parties were to be stoned, but of course, she was the only one brought before Jesus. Their plan was simple. If Jesus said she should be stoned, then the Pharisees could call Him out for convicting someone to death because only the Romans who ruled over Israel could issue a death sentence. But if He told them to let her go, the Pharisees could accuse Him of not acknowledging Moses' laws. Of course, in usual fashion, Jesus refused to argue and come down to their level. He could have told them they were already violating Moses' law by not including the other party involved, but instead He said nothing. He just knelt down in the dust and began to draw with His finger. Thinking Jesus was ignoring them, the Pharisees drew closer. As they came near, they saw what Jesus was writing.

All the while she sat in the dust with her head down and hair covering her face, not knowing what was happening because of Jesus' silence. She anticipated the first stone's sting. But finally He spoke, "Let he without sin cast the first stone." Thinking that any minute stones would rain down upon her, she almost felt a sense of release that no one could hurt her again, including herself. But instead there was silence, now by the Pharisees as well. She could hear footsteps and shuffling, but no words. With heavy hearts, all her accusers left one by one, from the oldest to the youngest. Their motive was not of justice and love. They had proudly entrapped this wounded woman and used her to trick Jesus, but their plan had backfired. They slinked away, convicted of their own wretchedness. When the woman was all alone with Jesus, He asked, "Woman, where are your accusers? Has no one condemned you?"

"No one, Lord," she said.

"Neither do I condemn you. Go and sin no more."

Never Forget His Love and Faithfulness

Tears fell from Mary's cheek onto her alabaster box as she thought about the faithful, rescuing love of Jesus, which not only saved her life physically, but also mentally and spiritually. Jesus cast seven demons out of Mary. His love and amazing grace, which was bestowed upon her in her most unfaithful moments, created in her a love for Him to which she thought she could never be capable. When Simon silently protested Mary's actions by thinking, *If only Jesus knew what manner this woman was, Jesus wouldn't allow her to touch Him,* Jesus replied to him, "But whoever has been forgiven little loves little. And whoever has been forgiven much, as Mary was forgiven much, loves much." We love Jesus because He first loved us. Focusing on Jesus and His love and patient faithfulness creates victory over our tendency to focus sinfully on ourselves.

He took away Mary's shame, which is the symptom of sin. Shame creates a self-centered perspective, and the more shame we feel the more we become a "me-monster." Sin is a prison cell made up of self and shame, which brings severe depression, negativity, addictions, and the constant comparing ones self to another (am I beautiful enough, am I more talented than he is, do I make more money than that person or drive a nicer car, etc.), all of which are self-centered actions.

The name Satan means accuser. It is not the Holy Spirit who accuses people and causes them to feel shame; it is Satan. The Holy Spirit prompts you to do what is right and convicts you of truth. Satan tempts and prompts people to taste destructive pleasures, and then he accuses them and oppresses them with shame and guilt, which can lead to more selfish, sinful acts. Many consciously and subconsciously believe Satan is out for their best interest, but Scripture reveals that "your enemy the devil prowls around like a roaring lion looking for someone to devour" (1 Peter 5:8, NIV).

Satan's ultimate fantasy for the human race is that he could make us replicas of the demoniacs from the region of Gerasenes. These madmen lived in tombs, cried out day and night, and cut themselves with stones. I imagine that these men looked like zombies, dirty, nasty, bloody, and mangled with mad eyes while screaming and attacking anyone who dared approach their stretch of shoreline. One look at these men running full speed at you, and you would run as if you had a rocket attached to your back. That's pretty much what the disciples did, but there existed no twinge of fear in Jesus as these men approached. The evil angels who had possessed these men were afraid of Jesus and thought He was there to torture them, thus proving the evil angels' perception of God's character. However, Jesus did not torture them; instead, he actually granted their wish to enter the heard of pigs nearby.

Satan had his hands on Mary and hoped he eventually would control her completely as he did the demoniacs of Gerasenes. But Jesus came to set everyone who was willing, such as Mary, free. Jesus' freedom brings about everything opposite of sin's symptoms. Love, peace, joy, and all the fruits of the Holy Spirit replace the zombie-like attributes Satan has instilled. Jesus sets us free as He did with Mary. And in our freedom, our true, beautiful character, which God created in us, is revealed and we learn exactly who we are and what will bring us true inner peace and joy. Remember, "what do you benefit if you gain the whole world but are yourself lost or destroyed?" (Luke 9:25, NLT).

When we follow sin and selfishness, we embark on a path of destruction, and during that journey, we lose our true selves. We think we are making our own choices and are doing as we please, but it is an illusion. We are in reality enslaved to accomplish Satan's bidding. All of who we are innately born to be is lost, and we become zombie clones of Satan and his selfish sadness. Satan disables and weakens and lazyfies (yep, I made up that word) the mind using any and every avenue possible, such as relaxing for hours in front of the TV or weakening our minds through alcohol or other addictive vices like pornography, which serves as a form of mind control. Most of our minds are so lazy that we cannot see a thought or project through to fruition. The plague of attention deficit disorder has swallowed up most people in first world countries.

There are infinite ways we allow Satan in, which consequently weakens our minds and pushes out the company and wisdom of God and His Holy Spirit and angels. All of Satan's deceptive marionette strings are disguised in a nice, neat package that makes it seem as though we are free-thinking individuals born to rebel against the mediocre. Before we realize it, we become clones, having a hive-like mentality with him pulling the strings. Satan doesn't care how he has or gets power, he just wants to be in control and worshiped. God is completely opposite, He desires loyalty by cognizant choice, not coercion. In Him, we reach our singularly unique full potential, mentally, physically, and spiritually. The closer we draw toward Jesus as a friend, the closer we move toward reaching Jesus-centered self-actualization, because

In Him, we reach our singularly unique full potential, mentally, physically, and spiritually.

the Creator who "began a good work in you will carry it on to completion until the day of Christ Jesus." Philippians 1:6 NIV.

Mary had experienced what it was like to be in bondage to Satan and there was no comparison to the freedom that comes through Jesus Christ. She was smitten with everything about Him and couldn't take her eyes off of Him. He became her One Thing, her Only Thing.

Mary, the party of one, possessed the most understanding of the true character of Jesus Christ and His mission. It was Mary's Jesus-focused eyes, heart and mind, which caused her understanding of Jesus' character and mission to be above and beyond any others. She loved Him unabashedly, and couldn't show enough appreciation for His gift of Himself. She entered the room where Jesus was sitting and began to poor the oil over His head. It ran down His hair and face and shoulders, onto His clothes and body. As she knelt before Jesus, she began to kiss his feet, and wipe the dirt off of them with her hair and tears. The effervescent fragrance delighted and drew everyone in, and by now all attention of those in Simon's home was focused on her and her offering. The Holy Spirit was using Mary and her offering to encourage Jesus during the darkest hours which were very soon to come. During His moments of anguish in complete separation from His Father, from the Garden of Gethsemane, to the walk to Golgatha and upon the cross, Jesus could smell the oil of spikenard with which Mary had anointed Him, the scent would have reminded Him of the appreciation, friendship and love of Mary and all others who loved Him as she did, that this darkest hour for Him would consummate eternity future for Mary and all who would be called His friend.

"Assuredly, I say to you, wherever this gospel is preached in the whole world, what this woman has done will also be told as a memorial to her." Mark 14:9 NKJV. Not only is Mary part of the gospel story that would be preached to the world throughout the end of the age, but she was the first person to see the risen Savior and was the first person to ever preach the gospel. See John 20:11–18. It is evident Mary's connection to Christ is an example for each and every person to follow.

You Hear but Do Not Understand

So how could it be possible that the disciples who walked with Jesus in the flesh for three and a half years and heard Him speak of His mission seemed to be confused as to the true mission and character of Jesus?

And how did the Pharisees and Sadducees and other Jewish religious leaders at the time of Jesus miss His arrival as the Messiah when they had the book of Daniel and its clear prophetic time prophesies? They knew the end of the 490-year prophecy was soon to be upon them because it is clear in Daniel that the start of the prophecy began at the going forth command to rebuild the temple, which was in 457 BC.

It is imperative we find the answers to these questions or we are doomed to history repeating itself in our own churches and hearts and minds. Jesus said He alone is the way, the truth and the life. I've gotten so tired of wasting my time reading and studying ideas and philosophies about God, religion, happiness, wisdom, education, love, health, and any other subject important to life only to find many rabbit holes lead to a dead end and thus more wasted time. So I went to the source of the one truth I know, the Bible, and I decided to study everything I could find in it about what it and Jesus teaches concerning truth so that I would make the most of my time in study and not miss important lessons and knowledge dangling right in front of my eyes. Many truths were right there in front of me throughout my life, but I missed them, just as the disciples had Jesus right there with them but they missed His point. Jesus' teachings were so simple, but they didn't understand Him or His mission.

The following are insightful texts in the Bible that speak about recognizing and knowing truth. Please read them carefully:

2 Corinthians 4:3, 4 – "If the Good News we preach is hidden behind a veil, it is hidden only from people who are perishing. Satan, who is the god of this world, has blinded the minds of those who don't believe. They are unable to see the glorious light of the Good News. They don't understand this message about the glory of Christ, who is the exact likeness of God" (NLT).

Matthew 13:10–15 – "His disciples came and asked him, 'Why do you use parables when you talk to the people?' He replied, 'You are permitted to understand the secrets of the Kingdom of Heaven, but others are not. To those who listen to my teaching, more understanding will be given, and they will have an abundance of knowledge. But for those who are not listening, even what little understanding they have will be taken away from them. That is why I use these parables, For they look, but they don't really see. They hear, but they don't really listen or understand. This fulfills the prophecy of Isaiah that says, "When you hear what I say, you will not understand. When you see what I do, you will not comprehend. For the hearts of these people are hardened, and their ears cannot hear, and they have closed their eyes—so their eyes cannot see, and their ears cannot hear, and their hearts cannot understand, and they cannot turn to me and let me heal them"'" (NLT).

Mark 6:52 – "For they still didn't understand the significance of the miracle of the loaves. Their hearts were too hard to take it in" (NLT).

Mark 8:16–21 – "At this they began to argue with each other because they hadn't brought any bread. Jesus knew what they were saying, so he said, 'Why are you arguing about having no bread? Don't you know or understand even yet? Are your hearts too hard to take it in? "You have eyes—can't you see? You have ears—can't you hear?" Don't you remember anything at all? When I fed the 5,000 with five loaves of bread, how many baskets of leftovers did you pick up afterward?' 'Twelve,' they said. 'And when I fed the 4,000 with seven loaves, how many large baskets of leftovers did you pick up?' 'Seven,' they said. 'Don't you understand yet?' he asked them" (NLT).

Luke 10:21 – "In that hour the Holy Spirit filled Jesus with joy. Jesus said, 'I praise you, Father, Lord of heaven and earth, for hiding these things from wise and intelligent people and revealing them to little children. Yes, Father, this is what pleased you'" (GW).

John 14:21 – "Whoever has my commands and keeps them is the one who loves me. The one who loves me will be loved by my Father, and I too will love them and show myself to them" (NIV).

Acts 5:32 – "We are witnesses of these things and so is the Holy Spirit, who is given by God to those who obey him" (NLT).

John 16:25 – "'I have said these things to you in figurative language. The time is coming when I will no longer speak to you in figurative language, but will tell you plainly about the Father. At that time, you will make your requests in my name, so that I will have no need to ask the Father on your behalf, because the Father himself loves you, and because you have loved me and believed that I came from God'" (ISV).

Numbers 12:1–8 – "While they were at Hazeroth, Miriam and Aaron criticized Moses because he had married a Cushite woman. They said, 'Has the Lord spoken only through Moses? Hasn't he spoken through us, too?' But the Lord heard them. (Now Moses was very humble—more humble than any other person on earth.) So immediately the Lord called to Moses, Aaron, and Miriam and said, 'Go out to the Tabernacle, all three of you!' So the three of them went to the Tabernacle. Then the Lord descended in the pillar of cloud and stood at the entrance of the Tabernacle. 'Aaron and Miriam!' he called, and they stepped forward. And the Lord said to them, 'Now listen to what I say: If there were prophets among you, I, the Lord, would reveal myself in visions. I would speak to them in dreams. But not with my servant Moses. Of all my house, he is the one I trust. I speak to him face to face, clearly, and not in riddles! He sees the Lord as he is. So why were you not afraid to criticize my servant Moses?'" (NLT).

John 14:26 – "But the Advocate, the Holy Spirit, whom the Father will send in my name, will teach you all things and will remind you of everything I have said to you" (NIV).

John 16:13 – "But when he, the Spirit of truth, comes, he will guide you into all the truth. He will not speak on his own; he will speak only what he hears, and he will tell you what is yet to come" (NIV).

Proverbs 3:5 – "Trust in the Lord with all thine heart; and lean not unto thine own understanding" (KJV).

Jeremiah 29:13 – "You will seek Me and find Me when you search for Me with all your heart" (NASB).

These verses are begging us to not have a theoretical relationship with God, or just an intelligent relationship of God; He wants a heart to heart, intimate relationship with us. The Holy Spirit and God alone lead to truth. Only by learning to invite God to walk moment by moment with us as a continual part of our daily lives can we truly know God and reap the benefits of being His friend, one of which is understanding truth. We can't expect to have a healthy marriage if we are barely spending any time with our spouse, and we can't have a close relationship with friends if we barely talk to them or spend time with them. The more time invested, the more we get to know in whom we are investing our time. The exact same rules apply to our relationship with Jesus. Reading Scripture once a day, even if it's just a verse, is a start, but more important than reading, we need to actually study the Bible by delving deep into all subjects, knowing the truth inside and out. God created us with brains to use. He wants us to believe because we've weighed the evidence and searched and compared all scriptures concerning each and every subject.

At the age of fifteen, I developed the habit of reading at least one verse in the Bible every day, and even during my most rebellious prodigal years, I mostly kept this habit. I suppose, perhaps, that this may have been what kept me from making even worse decisions than I did. But I wasn't truly investing my time, mind, and heart in the search to really know God. I was barely skimming by, doing just enough to ease my conscience.

When I met my husband and we began dating, he had barely begun his sea tour as a carrier pilot in the Navy. I was new to long-distance relationships, especially long-distance due to military deployments, so I had no idea what to expect, and neither did he. He was very excited to be deployed, live abroad, travel, and do what he had been trained to do. Therefore, one of the last things on his mind was communicating with me or anyone else. Although he was a carrier pilot, this first deployment was a land based assignment, which is completely different than a carrier based deployment because he had his own room with Internet and plenty of free time.

Despite the fact that he could communicate easily via the Internet with me during the initial part of his deployment, I barely heard from him. If I was lucky, I maybe got an email a day. Consequently we began to lose touch, but

I decided that before I'd give up on the relationship I'd let him know I wished we could visit more. Being the awesome man he is, he came up with creative ways for us to spend time together. We had movie dates on Skype. I'd cue up a movie on my end, and he'd cue up the same movie on his end, and we'd start the movies at the exact same time so we could watch it "together," then we'd talk about anything and everything over video chat. Day after day, and with each week, we found we were talking and spending longer and longer hours visiting.

The point of this diatribe is that an e-mail here and there wasn't going to encourage our relationship to grow, just as reading a verse in the Bible here and there and saying a quick passing prayer won't allow for growth in our relationship

The key to continual growth in any relationship is to never ever become stagnant.

with Jesus. If we operate this way, we are selling ourselves short because there are so many beautiful truths and a deeper knowledge of Jesus Christ that we are missing. When we search the Scriptures and study and come and reason with God as He asks us, we step into a whole new world. The key to continual growth in any relationship is to never ever become stagnant.

In today's world, Satan uses technology and the overstimulation of media to distract us from perceiving truth. Our brains are constantly being told what to think about. And the media is constantly telling us what we should want and like. It has been said that the average adult has the potential to be exposed to about 600–625 ads a day through television, radio, the Internet, billboards, and any other means of media advertising. Under these circumstances, we are easily distracted and easily influenced and deceived.

The only way to not be blinded by these layers of deception is to put on Jesus' X-ray vision glasses. If we begin to study and choose truth, Jesus takes away Satan's ability to blind us. The power lies in choice—Jesus and the angels are in angst waiting for us to make the choice to allow the power of God to permeate every aspect of our lives.

Sin in essence is selfishness and the focus on one's self and this seemingly default state of mind of self-centeredness is such an easy deception that clouds our perceptions of reality. Focusing on ourselves will always be a stumbling block between us and Jesus and any other relationship we may pursue. The problem is that most of us don't even realize when we are being selfish. For instance, one of the examples of the disciples' hearts not fully being open to truth was when the Samaritan villagers rejected Jesus, and the disciples asked Jesus if they should call fire down from heaven (see Luke 9:51–56). Jesus rebuked them harshly for this, saying, "Ye know not what manner of spirit ye are of" (verse 55, KJV). When we criticize others, even if it appears they most certainly deserve it as in the case with the Samaritan villagers, we are presuming we are good enough to judge them, which in turn is saying we are better than them because of our own good works. But we need to realize that if it weren't for the grace of God we'd be capable of anything our worst enemy is capable of.

The deception that Satan wants us to believe in this area is that salvation lies in ourselves through our own good deeds and behavior. If we love almost everyone but harbor hate against only one person no matter what awful sin he/she committed against us, then we truly cannot be a converted person who loves God. Being judgmental and selfish is not modeling the love of Jesus. This does not mean we have to like what that person has done and keep being a victim. It doesn't mean we have to spend time with them, but it means we should not burn with hate for them in our hearts, which only eats us up inside and destroys our health and happiness. Instead we need to tell God about our anger and talk with Him about how we feel.

When we turn things over to God and share our thoughts and feelings through prayer, it allows Him to fully work in the situation. Over the years I've prayed for my enemies, those who have hurt me and lied about me. I've complained to God about these people and turned the circumstances of our relationship over to Him. What has amazed me is that He has worked to bring us together at a later stage. A number of my former "enemies" are now close friends, and one is even a best friend. The healing of hearts and relationships in the most grievous of circumstances is one of the most powerful examples of God's existence and power. We live in selfishness, but when we turn things over to God, He can change a selfish heart into a loving heart. And there's a freedom and joy in that that's unsurpassed because the power to change a hardened human heart is greater evidence of the power of God than if we were to say to a mountain, "Move," and it moved.

Jesus had performed this miracle in the heart of Mary Magdalene; He healed her heart, and she reclaimed her identity. She thought she was beyond anyone's capability to help; she thought there was no way out, but Jesus was capable, although she knew she didn't deserve rescuing. She saw in Jesus' faithfulness, her unfaithfulness and unworthiness, and she didn't dare pass judgment on anyone else because she knew what it was like to be the focus of downward stares. She realized her dark heart could not be trusted and she needed a Savior. But the disciples didn't quite fully recognize their sinful natures and their need of a Savior. They had preconceived notions and had bought into many of the deceptive teachings of the religious leaders at that time. The Pharisees and Sadducees and other Jewish leaders thought themselves to be beyond holy and awesome. Their whole religious system was based on working their way to becoming holy. Any conviction in their hearts by the Holy Spirit was almost immediately squashed by their motivation to gain more control and power. Righteousness by works is an indication that we want to be in control and not let God be in control of our lives.

Mary was willing to accept the fact that she was a sinner in need of a Savior. She didn't try to hide this truth. She remembered what happened to her life when she insisted on being in control, so she let go and let God guide her in His wisdom. Jesus thanked the Father in Luke 10:21 for hiding the truth from those who think they are wise and intelligent and who think they can be saved on their own accord and for revealing truth to those who were like children, who know they are incapable of being successful by leaning on their own wisdom. Children depend on their parents for survival. So the secret behind Mary's success was that she was like a little child. She realized more than anyone else, even more that the disciples, that she needed her Jesus. He was the "One Thing" that could save her from herself.

Our job, according to Jesus, is to believe in and be thankful for Jesus' gift to us, and then we are to seek and emulate His true character and introduce others to Him. "And this gospel of the kingdom will be preached in the whole world as a testimony to all nations, and then the end will come" (Matt. 24:14, NIV). The only way this will be fully possible is through the help of the Holy Spirit. If we are not seeking, searching, and studying with a sincere desire to know the truth of Jesus, we are going to be distracted and miss all the warning signs Jesus gave us about His soon return, and we will be deceived just as the Pharisees and Sadducees were. Mary made Jesus her one thing. The only way we can thrive and discern what is truth and survive the last days before Jesus' return is to follow her example. "For false messiahs and false prophets will appear and perform great signs and wonders to deceive, if possible, even the elect" (verse 24, NIV).

To be continued in the next chapter ...

Chapter 5

Reflection of Truth: A Most Humbling Experience

For the first thirty years of my life, I was no stranger to embarrassing moments. They seemed to happen often and at the most inconvenient times. My face still turns bright red and I shutter even decades later at the thought of a few of them.

About fifteen years ago, I was to perform a song in front of hundreds of people at church. I was up next in the program, but I desperately needed to use the restroom. I flew to the bathroom, but because I was in a hurry, I failed to look at myself in the mirror before I left the restroom. I immediately found myself on the receiving end of some lingering stares and snickering, but because my mind was on getting to the back of the stage as soon as possible, I blew it off and raced down the hall to the back entrance of the stage. As I proceeded down the hallway, a friend abruptly stopped me and informed me I had a code red situation that needed to be immediately addressed. I asked what he meant, and he cleared his throat and said, "Look at the back of your dress." I quickly turned my head and realized that the back of my dress was stuck in the top of my pantyhose (yes, women wore hosiery back then), revealing my backside and panties. To make matters much worse, the toilet seat protector happened to be dangling nicely out of the top of my hosiery as the ultimate pinnacle ornament of embarrassment. There were several people who saw me in this compromised situation. I was so thankful my friend stopped me before I had made it to the stage! I would have passed out from embarrassment.

Many times in our lives we don't notice the egg on our own faces until someone points it out. We often buy into deception, deceit, traditions, and philosophies because we're raised to or told to—we don't even question our perceived realities. But if we would take time and stop and look in the mirror, we would see that we have something dangling from our pantyhose that is quite embarrassing. Fortunately, the Bible is the friend who alerts us to our embarrassing situation and provides a solution. It outlines what truth is in life. The character of God and His Ten Commandments are a mirror that reflects and reveals to us our weaknesses and our desperate need for a Savior who is the only One capable of removing our shame by replacing it with His glory.

Dare To Be a Maverick

Red pill or blue pill?

Like the character Neo in the movie *The Matrix,* we are all faced with the decision to choose or not to choose reality. Many consciously or subconsciously wish to remain as sheeple, people who exhibit a herd mentality such as sheep, following the crowd and their subtly force-fed mainstream ideals, philosophies, and thoughts. They refuse to think because they are lazy or scared of the truth and its conclusions, so they seemingly remain blissfully ignorant.

If something is ninety-nine percent truth and one percent false, it is still a deception.

Much of our beliefs about religion, ethics, sociology, psychology, and the like are the result of our exposure to the media in all its forms and the talking heads who endorse the educated authorities. Without even being cognizant of it, we have become non-independent thinkers because much of our stream of consciousness is force-fed to us by the media.

Satan is very subtle in deceptions. Many are ninety-nine percent truths, mixed with one percent error, and he does this with all subjects, especially theology. If something is ninety-nine percent truth and one percent false, it is still a deception. The most grievous aspect of Satan's plethora of deceptions is that most all of them vilify God and give us a hideous perspective of who He is.

When the disciples asked what the sign of Jesus' coming would be and the end of the age, Jesus immediately warned them to not be deceived. We are living in a time where we are inundated with deception; it is almost impossible to discern truth from all the lies. Deception has invaded every part of our life, and Jesus said it will get worse before He returns. Only a vital connection and focus on God will push out of sight the deception with which Satan attempts to block our vision.

Humans have succumbed and embraced deception since we believed the first lie told to us by Lucifer. Because Adam and Eve believed him, they effectively invited him and his ways to be a part of our existence. Jesus called him the prince of this world and the father of lies. His likeness brings shame and defensiveness. Excuses and lies are then made to ease our guilty consciences or to prevent others from thinking poorly of us, which further aggravates our guilty conscience. There are many reasons we lie, and after thousands of generations of liars begetting liars, lying has become reflexive. Many of us lie without realizing it or with no premeditation. Robert Feldman at the University of Massachusetts conducted an experiment to see just how reflexive and second nature lying is for humans. Feldman picked two strangers from his subjects to talk to each other for ten minutes in each session. Most individuals said they did not lie during the conversation, but when the subjects reviewed the recording they were astounded at the number of tiny lies they had actually told in the ten-minute period. Lies they weren't even aware they had told. It was concluded that an average of 2.92 lies were told within the ten-minute experiment. Our first lies are usually told around the age of two or three, and by the time we are an adult, according to Wikipedia, the average woman lies between one and five times a day and the average man lies between three and nine times a day.

To not be deceived, we should not deceive. If we make it our goal and ask Jesus to help keep our lips from lying, we will become increasingly aware of our words and begin to think before we speak. It is extremely freeing to experience this. When we stop lying, it's as if a huge weight is lifted off of us, and it's a characteristic of God's true followers, especially the elect of the last days of earth's history when Jesus said deception would exist on an epic scale. "They follow the Lamb wherever he goes.... No lie was found in their mouths; they are blameless" (Rev. 14:4, 5, NIV). "He will use all sorts of displays of power through signs and wonders that serve the lie, and all the ways that wickedness deceives those who are perishing. They perish because they refused to love the truth and so be saved" (2 Thess. 2:9, 10, NIV). King David wrote about those who may come into the presence of the Lord: "Who may climb the mountain of the Lord? Who may stand in his holy place? Only those whose hands and hearts are pure, who do not worship idols and never tell lies. They will receive the Lord's blessing and have a right relationship with God their savior" (Ps. 24:3–5, NLT).

The only way to become a truthful person and to get rid of deception is by focusing on Jesus. As Revelation 14:4 said, those who will overcome will do so by following the Lamb wherever He goes. In practical life terms, that means when we go to work, we think about the pardoning love and grace of Jesus and anything and everything that pertains to Him. Because I am looking, I see God's essence in almost every place and activity I find myself in. When we are with our spouse, or cooking dinner, or going to a birthday party, or playing a baseball game, or riding roller coasters at Six Flags, or body surfing in Hawaii, or running a 5K, or driving, we can invite Jesus and His holy angels into our bubble. We can experience a taste of heaven right now by continually inviting Jesus and the Holy Spirit and His angels into every activity we find ourselves in, which plants Him deeper into our hearts and minds.

When Kris and I are apart, we usually are texting or calling each other. We may send pictures of the food we are eating or the view from our hotel room or the friends we are with. Even though we are apart, we are inviting the other into our adventure at that time by including, to some degree, each other in the little details of our day. This makes us feel like we are not missing out as much on each other's company. It is the same way with God and prayer or remembrance of scriptures I read at an earlier time that pertain to a certain event that happened during the day. I find myself talking to God throughout my day even about seemingly insignificant details, but that's the thing, to God they are not insignificant, just as the ambiance of a restaurant Kris is at is not insignificant to me.

If I'm at a restaurant and I see an act of honesty or kindness by a stranger to a server, I thank God. If I see someone verbally mistreating another, I pray for them and talk to God about it. If I'm listening to the radio and hear a beautiful voice, I thank God for blessing that person with that gift because they in turn are blessing me with their gift. If I feel lonely, I tell God how I feel. If I feel happy, I thank God. If I'm angry, I talk to God about it. Communicating with Kris when we are apart brings him close to me despite our physical distance. Communicating with God even though we are physically apart now brings Him closer and closer to us until He is enthroned in our hearts. Jesus said in Luke 17:21: "You see, the kingdom of God is within you" (GW).

Unfortunately, when we knowingly choose to sin and participate in deception, we invite Satan into our hearts and minds. God is knocking; He desperately wants to come in and push Satan out, but when we ignore Him, His knocks become more and more muffled as we sink further into darkness. We sin every day without even realizing it, but it is the cherished, known sins we harbor in our hearts and souls that in effect communicates to Satan that we are choosing him. We were created free moral agents. Because of Jesus' law of love, He cannot go against those love principles; He must respect our choices.

I wish I had known fifteen years ago what I know now. Maybe I wouldn't have been as easily deceived by others and by my own selfish heart. My prayer is that you, by reading this book, can at least avoid some of the deceptions and avoid many of the mistakes I made.

I have devoted the rest of this chapter to laying out before you some of the most sneaky and prevalent deceptions of our time in the simplest ways I know how. I urge you to please do your own research on these topics and on everything I have written. And remember to pray before you seek truth so that the Holy Spirit is leading you and not another spirit.

Just Follow Your Heart

I have made more mistakes in my lifetime buying into this philosophy than any other deceptive way of thinking. Thank you, Disney. Seriously, they have been selling this concept, making it a ginormous part of pop-culture, for the last ninety years. Much of their glamorous movie themes and storylines are predicated on this notion.

This mindset leads down a dirty and dark road, "The heart *is* deceitful above all *things,* And desperately wicked; Who can know it?" (Jer. 17:9, NKJV).

Our hearts and minds are naturally bent toward selfishness. We all begin our lives consumed with selfish ambitions. Our natural inclinations always lean toward selfishness and self-preservation.

Only through the Holy Spirit will we gain an understanding of selfless living. The Holy Spirit helps us fight against the natural inclinations of sinfulness. Paul says it perfectly, "For I don't do the good I want to do, but instead do the evil that I don't want to do" (Rom. 7:19, ISV).

Making decisions based upon what feels good or right will often steer us wrong. Many relationships have been sabotaged by the "just follow your heart" mantra. Many of us impulsively make life-changing decisions with this notion as our guiding light. Um … no! This is so wrong. Only the Holy Spirit leads people into all truth and light. Bad things will still happen in life no matter what, but much of our own self inflicted times of hell would be avoided if we would sincerely pray and seek guidance from the Holy Spirit instead of impulsively doing what feels right at the time. Esau was a perfect example of this. He was willing to impulsively give up his birthright to Jacob over a bowl of stew because he was hungry and desired instant gratification. It "felt" good in that moment, but he had no regard for the future outcome of his decision.

Eloquently, Paul says in Romans, "Those who let themselves be controlled by their lower natures live only to please themselves, but those who follow after the Holy Spirit find themselves doing those things that please God. Following after the Holy Spirit leads to life and peace, but following after the old nature leads to death because the old sinful nature within us is against God. It never did obey God's laws and it never will. That's why those who are still under the control of their old sinful selves, bent on following their old evil desires, can never please God" (Rom. 8:5–8, TLB).

Certain aspects of this way of thinking have worked their way into Christianity. We wind up rejecting certain truths or ways that are light because they don't evoke a nostalgic feeling or because they are just plain inconvenient to accept. It seems that many times Christians lose interest if they aren't experiencing a feeling of nostalgia and forced "holy spirit" highs. But we should all be seeking truth. God's voice sometimes comes in big booming epic announcements wrought with impact. But many times He comes in the still small voice as He did with Elijah in the cave when he was hiding from Jezebel.

A relationship with God is not about a feeling, or a high, or "what can God do for me"; it is about a relationship with the person who is God. We have the highest privilege in the universe to intimately know Elohim. If we truly understood the awesomeness of this privilege, all else would be counted as nothing in comparison. To develop a relationship and know a person, or even an animal, it takes an incredible amount of patience and time. Many times there is no "good feeling" involved. In fact, the opposite feelings may be involved, but through perseverance and loyalty, we begin to gain the highs of our investments of time and patience. This process is completely opposite of the "just follow your heart" idea. Many times in life, and especially relationships, what we want to do, we shouldn't, and what we don't want to do, we should, and just because we can doesn't mean we should. "Don't worry about anything; instead, pray about everything. Tell God what you need, and thank him for all he has done. Then you will experience God's peace, which exceeds anything we can understand. His peace will guard your hearts and minds as you live in Christ Jesus" (Phil. 4:6, 7, NLT).

Remember, if there is any theology that contradicts the message that God is love, then more study is required because that theology is false.

There has been a lot of talk recently about the ecumenical movement, which is the movement to unite all Christians (Catholics and Protestants) into one body. I love unification. I yearn for unification. The thought of unification moves me to a happy place, as I'm sure it does most everyone who fantasizes about it. People despise being alone because we were made to have relationships with others. But we need to be sure we are uniting with people, whether they are in our own church or other churches, in truth, not uniting just because it feels good to be unified in "brotherly love."

Some of the biggest mistakes I've made in my life were because I decidedly made awful choices to save face and please those to whom I had undeservingly given my loyalties. We should all have brotherly love for everyone, even those we know who are teaching deception. We should pray for them earnestly and not harbor hatred or animosity, but this doesn't mean we have to hang out with them and be their best friend and promote them. Being cautious of someone's teachings is not being unloving, it is being wise as serpents and gentle as doves.

The human heart is so fickle. Most of us don't even know what we truly want. Often times when we get what we want, happiness and fulfillment do not follow. There is one individual who knows us better than anyone else and better than we know ourselves, that is our Creator. He is all-knowing and all-powerful, He is everywhere at all times throughout the universe. He is also all loving. He knows the beginning from the end. His wisdom, not our own, should be trusted. "Trust in the Lord with all your heart and lean not on your own understanding" (Prov. 3:5, NIV).

A Loving God Can't Exist When There Is So Much Pain

"When someone has been given much, much will be required in return; and when someone has been entrusted with much, even more will be required" (Luke 12:48, NLT).

You've no doubt heard of the saying "acts of God." When a hurricane, tornado, tsunami, or any other natural disaster happens, the first person people blame is God as if He was angry and made it happen. This mentality has actually been adopted into most cultural ways of thinking from pagan belief systems—the notion that "the gods are angry so we must appease them." The Bible is full of evidence of this way of thinking in Jesus' time and even much earlier than that in Old Testament times, such as in the book of Job. If someone was born with an illness, or struck with an illness such as Job, it was automatically assumed that he or his parents committed some sin against God so he was being punished (see Job and John 9).

But Jesus made it clear in John 9 that the man whom He healed was not being punished for sins he or his parents committed. It most certainly was not an act of God or His will. Some translations of the Bible elude that he was born blind for the purpose of Jesus performing a miracle to show His power, but in the original Greek, it was written to the effect that this man was born blind and Jesus healed him, but God did not ordain this man to be born blind so Jesus could work a miracle.

It is very important to research and study the original Hebrew and Greek texts because sometimes phrases have lost their true meaning through various translations. For instance, in the story of Joseph as it appears in Genesis, it is mentioned many times that God hardened Pharaoh's heart so He could unleash the ten plagues against Egypt. But God did not coldly and heartlessly force the king of Egypt to disbelieve. The king chose to not believe, and because he would not repent, he was blinded from the truth. This theme is repeated throughout the Bible.

Recent Bible movies have picked up on this incorrect coldness and have even tried to make people feel sorry for Judas. The view is that someone had to betray Jesus and Judas drew the short straw. But if someone such as Judas or Pharaoh truly had a repentant heart and was open to the love of God, they would not have been blinded to the truth. God desperately desires all to be saved and to experience His freedom, so if an individual even shows an inkling of hope in Him, He will not let them go and will lead them into truth.

Remember, if there is any theology that contradicts the message that God is love, then more study is required because that theology is false. God does not cause natural disasters, and it is not God's will for anyone to be ill or die. It is because of Satan and our choices that bad things happen to us and to this world. We were given dominion over this world, but when we chose Satan to be our ruler, we chose for all the innocent creatures and creation of this earth to be subject to Satan's destructive power. The fact of the matter is that if it weren't for God no one would even be alive, much less have any semblance of happiness.

The human race has been degenerating since sin entered the DNA chain through Adam and Eve. We now exist as a shell of what we were originally created to be. Diseases and hereditary and cultivated tendencies have over-taken the human race, but none of this was God's will, and one day no more death or disease or crying will exist. One day very soon.

Many who don't believe in God say they cannot believe in a higher power because they'd rather believe there is no God than believe there is a God who does not intervene when He is perfectly capable of ending and preventing sorrow, pain, and death. Then again, even out of those who believe there is a Creator many still don't understand how there can be such darkness.

God, who is the originator of love, gives us a choice to love and honor Him and obey His sinless, life-giving ways. True love is strictly voluntary. You cannot force someone to love you; it completely defies the definition of love. With great power (love) comes great responsibility. If God just forced everyone to follow Him and do His bidding, then we'd be loveless drones. We are responsible for our own actions, and if we don't live up to that responsibility, then sin takes hold, and we bring pain and devastation upon others and ourselves, sometimes in unimaginable ways. The more the Holy Spirit and His fruits of love abide in our inmost being, the less we will be capable of wronging others.

Jesus shared an insightful parable relating to the sin problem in Matthew 13:24–30. He tells of a farmer who planted wheat in his field, but at night as the workers slept, an enemy came and planted weeds among the wheat. As the crop grew, so did the weeds. The workers ran to the farmer, told him that the good seed was full of weeds, and asked him where it came from. The farmer replied, "An ENEMY has done this."

"Should we pull the weeds?" the workers asked.

"No," replied the farmer, "you'll uproot the wheat if you do."

The farmer represents Christ, the enemy is Satan, the workers are God's followers, the weeds are sin, and the wheat is all of Christ's beloved creation. Notice that Jesus said an "enemy" did this. Planting the weeds was not an act of the farmer or Christ. And although it made perfect sense to the workers to pull the weeds from the tender seedlings, Jesus said that it would hurt and uproot the wheat to do so. Pain, death, darkness, distress, anguish, and disease are all caused by Satan—he is the enemy of life.

Unfortunately, if God had uprooted sin when Satan had rebelled in heaven or immediately after Eve ate the fruit, then all of God's creation, including the angels, would have served him out of fear instead of love, and the good wheat would have been uprooted with the weeds. First John 4:18 says, "Perfect love expels all fear" (NLT).

Satan's claim that Christ is unfair has been a common deceptive theme. It was whispered into the ears of the angels, and a third of them believed the lie and were cast from heaven. And he has been whispering it into the ears of all generations since the first couple. Before Christ returns, Satan will have fully shown his true intentions for humanity, and those intentions will be fully recognized for their destructive nature. Until Satan's true character is realized and Christ's true character is vindicated, God cannot intervene and end this great controversy. All must see Satan for who he really is: "our great enemy, the devil. He prowls around like a roaring lion, looking for someone to devour" (1 Peter 5:8, NLT).

Until Satan's true character is realized and Christ's true character is vindicated, God cannot intervene and end this great controversy.

Satan has deceived us into believing his ways are the path to freedom, knowledge, fame, wealth, power, pleasure, and happiness. He has tricked us into believing that he is our friend, not enemy, because he can give us what makes us feel good. There may be a short time of perceived pleasure but sin's honeymoon phase is short lived, and we soon realize that the perceived pleasures were really slavery, empty, and meaningless.

After the great controversy between Christ and Satan has ended and we are finally given eternal life, we and the angels will still have the freedom to love God or rebel against Him, but because all who have chosen life have seen the true face and fruition of sin's despair, no one will choose to give up the paradise that was restored. "Affliction will not rise up a second time" (Nahum 1:9, NKJV). Christ's eternal scars, which will be visible in His hands and feet and side, will be a reminder of the cost of our freedom from sin, sorrow, sadness, and death. How would we be able to deny such incomparable love? We won't be able to. "He will wipe every tear from their eyes, and there will be no more death or sorrow or crying or pain. All these things are gone forever" (NLT). We will sing unending praise to our Savior.

The Theory of Evolution

I must begin by pointing out that this is a theory, not scientific fact, but it is taught as an irrefutable fact that we are the descendants of a last universal common ancestor (microbial bacteria), a process that began some 3.8 million years ago. The arguments for this theory are well crafted and seem to have the support of the scientific world. The following are thoughts that make me go *hmmm* concerning this theory;

The fossil record shows life just came onto the scene, which is what scientists call the Cambrian Explosion. Animals and plant fossils just appeared seemingly out of nowhere. There is no evidence of a gradual increase in complexity and size of the animals and fauna. It's as though an intelligent being spoke into existence life, in all its grandeur. Life wasn't and then it was.

"Scientists" have reported to have seen evidence of flightless birds being hatched from reptile eggs in the dinosaur fossil record. They also say scientists have found evidence in the fossil record of the transition of reptile to mammals and ape to humans. They have also found what scientists recognize as a legged whale and legged sea cow. When I have researched and read over the information scientists list as proof of evolution and so-called transitional species, I am confused by the notion these findings are proof of anything. We don't witness for ourselves in our current time, a collard lizard hatching a scarlet macaw, so if we only have ghosts of faint supposed evidence in the past that is not necessarily being observed today, how do we know for sure that what they think they are seeing is the factual interpretation. The major problem with this finding of supposed evidence is that it is a self-reinforcing pretense of "scientific truth." Scientists act as though all evidence found in the fossil record supports the theory of evolution, in effect, suggesting that it is non-falsifiable, or it is a tautology. But for any scientific theory to be proven and become fact, it must be falsifiable. All possible interpretations for a scientific finding must be considered and tested before a conclusion is drawn. The first step in the scientific method is to observe the studied phenomenon.

The problem with the theory of evolution, namely macroevolution, is we do not observe it today and it is not an experiment one can reproduce in a laboratory, so the third step of the scientific method is also a no-go for this theory because it is not observable or repeatable. So why is this taught as a scientific fact? There is no absolute, refutable, observable evidence for the change of kinds. We see microevolution, which is a change within species; however, there is no real, concrete observable evidence of macroevolution, which is major changes of whole groups of species. We do not even definitively see this within the fossil record.

Carl Sagan, at a SETI (search for extraterrestrial intelligence) conference, presented a paper that estimated the odds of a single specific human genome spontaneously assembling as being 1 in $10 \char`^ 2,000,000,000$. He along with many other scientists recognize the improbability of a human genome assembling at random, but they still refuse to believe in the God of all true science and creation. Some hold to the theory that all life on our planet was deposited by an alien race.

Life never spontaneously generates. All species are said to have come from one common ancestor. OK, well let's just say for augment's sake that everything about macroevolution is true and we evolved from one common ancestor. So, the ten billion dollar question is, where did the universal common ancestor come from? Louis Pasteur disproved the theory of spontaneous generation in the mid-nineteenth century with his sterile broth experiment. It is not a natural occurrence for life to come from nothing, the belief that spontaneous genesis was our origin is not true science because it is a supernatural belief, yet scientists argue against Creation being an option of our origins because it is a supernatural belief. Either side takes faith, and I would argue that there is more evidence we were created by an intelligent Creator, than we evolved from some uni-cellular organism millions or billions of years in the past that sponta-neously generated from primordial soup. My iPhone is infinitely less complex than one cell in my body, yet I know my iPhone had a group of intelligent Apple Company masterminds, the perfect ingredients didn't fall into a pile and spontaneously assimilate into a fully functioning mini computer.

Recognizing Pasteur's scientific evidence as fact, scientists thought up a new, but similar, theory to spontaneous generation that questions the origin of life. They call it abiogenesis. Spontaneous generation is the belief that life as we see it today, even microbial life, spontaneously appeared from beef broth or other rotting garbage. But abiogenesis predicts that the essential components were in place millions of years ago to begin a chemical chain reaction and the chemical components of life self-arranged because of perfect conditions, and thus biology came out of chemistry with the chemical chain reactions essential for the building blocks of life, amino acids, then forming. How probable is this theory? Yes, it is possible, but it is absolutely improbable. Just as it is improbable for these perfect conditions and ingredients to occur, it is almost as improbable, if not more so, for the immensely complex machines that are cells to somehow gain genetic information, which over time and by chance could become a chicken heart cell, or a zebra brain cell, or a human muscle cell, or an eagle's eye cell.

When it comes right down to it, theists and atheists alike require a certain amount of faith to go on to hold onto their beliefs, for neither side has irrefutable evidence. We can always think our way out of any hypothesis; therefore, regurgitating a list of inconsistencies will not necessarily convert a person's mind or heart. "Belief is a wise wager. Granted that faith cannot be proved, what harm will come to you if you gamble on its truth and it proves false? If you gain, you gain all; if you lose, you lose nothing. Wager, then, without hesitation, that He exists," said Blaise Pascal, a French philosopher speaking of the belief in God. This is an argument often cited by theists, but it is a wise argument, and what would be the harm in experimenting with a relationship with God.

There have been times in my life when I've questioned whether God existed or if He even cared, and at one point, I did take on many atheistic scientific beliefs, but over time I couldn't argue myself out of the fact that I knew I had a relationship with Jesus Christ. Even though I cannot see Him or physically touch Him, the evidence of His involvement in my life was as concrete as the evidence my mother exists and is involved in my life. No one can prove to me my mother doesn't exist. Personal testimony to God's existence is one of the proofs He is real, now multiply that by billions of people who believe in God and who, throughout history, have believed in God. It's possible we all could be crazy, but not probable. A true philosopher or scientist seeks absolute truth. If you are an atheist with the spirit of a true philosopher or scientist who is seeking absolute truth and you are reading this book, I challenge you to an experiment. Start with a prayer; ask God if He exists; tell Him you feel crazy talking to Him; tell Him whatever you are thinking; but also tell Him you want to know the truth. Then incorporate some sort of exchange with God every day. Start by reading the gospel of John, then Genesis, then the rest of the New Testament and Psalms and Proverbs, and finally the remaining books of the Bible. Even if you don't make it that far, even if you just make it a week or a month, keep a journal and see if you recognize the presence and existence of Elohim in your heart and mind.

A thread of atheism has existed throughout most of human history, but it was ignited with fury in 1789 as a revolt to the oppression and obscurity from truth that was created because of the unification of papal Rome and the monarchies of Europe and their lust for power. Finally, fed up with the hundreds of years of power hungry church leaders, the French Revolution and the beginnings of modern atheism was born. I suspect I would have been an atheist too. There is no way I could have loved and served the tyrannical god to which the people were forced to submit.

The philosophy of atheism took on a new form and grew in popularity after the publication of *The Origin of Species* by Charles Darwin in 1859. Since then the theory of evolution and Darwinism has been woven into the fiber of everyday life, coloring our interpretation of others and ourselves, including human actions and emotions and everything in the world around us. Many theists have morphed this theory in with their creation beliefs, which is dangerous because it undermines God's intimate involvement in creating humans. This also means death would have existed before Adam and Eve were created and were deceived to rebel, which would mean the wages of sin is not death. It also diminished God's creative power of a literal six days of Creation, with the seventh being the temple of time—the Sabbath, the day of rest. God could have chosen to speak everything into existence in a nanosecond, but He chose to create our universe, its laws of physics that govern it, the earth and everything in it, including the seven day week time period, in seven days.

Survival of the fittest and death were not a part of the creation plan for humans, animals, or plants. We were created to live forever, but we chose to believe Satan and separate ourselves from God, the author of life, which leads to death. God was intimate in creating humans, He formed us with His own hands and pressed His lips to our mouth and nose and breathed into us the breath of life. And He is still seeking, pursuing, and desiring that intimate connection with us. We just keep running away and allowing Satan to block our view with his distractions and deceit.

Because atheism, Darwinism, the theory of evolution, and anything of the like have become such a mainstream way of thinking, it has caused many people, even Christians, to rationalize certain immoral behaviors. For instance, we live in a highly sexualized society. It's everywhere we look. I've read that for every normal website on the Internet there are several porn sites. It's crazy sick, and it's readily available on our iPhones, tablets, laptops, iPods, etc. It's all at our fingertips, and most men and women and married couples think it's normal to look at these sites. When people believe they are just evolved animals, it's easier to take on animalistic behaviors like being promiscuous and indulging in every fantasy one can think of. Evolution scientists tell us we can't help it because it's our innate drive to propagate the human species. And aspects of this brainwashing have crept into Christianity.

I should not have to tell you how demoralizing this view is on so many levels. Pornography devalues the meaning of sex; it devalues women and their artistically, God-designed bodies. It also devalues men, and it devalues the marriage relationship, which is a symbolism of Christ's relationship with us. And ultimately it corrupts people's minds. It is severely addictive and ruins relationships. God made sex to be a pleasing experience between a husband and wife, He created it as a way for a couple to grow in oneness and closeness, mentally and physically, not as a selfish act where people just want,

want, want. Satan has completely perverted sex, which has corrupted many marriage relationships and families. Many people are slaves to sex and have bought into the lie that it is all about pleasing themselves and no one else.

Radiometric Dating

It's hard science, right? Many different radioactive isotopes exist in our world, and they decay at a certain rate that produces a daughter isotope or a decay product. We presume the decay rates have remained constant throughout this earth's history. Thus we deduce that this decaying process can give us insight into the age of almost any matter we find. It sounds so simple and makes absolute sense, but when you look at the variables involved with radiometric dating, questions arise.

Christians estimate from the genealogies listed in the Bible that the earth is about 6,000 years old. This drastically differs from how old scientists say the earth is—approximately 4.54 billion years. They arrive at this date from the radiometric dating of meteorite fragments. I use to wonder if Adam and Eve were in the garden for quite some time before they sinned and that's why the radiometric results were so old. Then I thought maybe God created our universe before He formed the earth, and then He used components from His already existing universe to form the earth and our solar system, thus giving us an old age earth.

Some theologians think that perhaps the stars and the rest of the universe were created at another earlier time and on the fourth day, as documented by Moses in Genesis, the stars were allowed to be seen and give light to the earth through the firmament from the heavens. Some also believe, because of 2 Peter 3:8, that the day period in Genesis 1 is not a literal twenty-four hour period of time. But applying that verse to the Creation account is false.

The Hebrew word *yom*, which means day, clearly denotes it is as a literal twenty-four-hour time period because it is sequenced by saying there was the evening and the morning, which was the first day. *Yom* usually means a twenty-four-hour period when it is qualified with a number. The fact we have a seven-day week that has remained throughout human history despite attempts to change it also proves the reasonability of a literal seven-day creation week. He also blessed the seventh-day and sanctified it. It wouldn't make sense to bless a day if it was an ambiguous amount of time. Also, time itself, a phenomenon scientists, philosophers, and theologians cannot adequately understand or explain, is a clue to our being created, not evolved.

Genesis 1:1 begins with "in the beginning," which means God created the concept of time. This creation of time is further expounded on a few verses later when describing the creation of the fourth day when God created the sun, moon, and stars, which were to "be lights in the firmament of the heavens to divide the day from the night; and let them be for signs and seasons, and for days and years" (verse 14, NKJV). One thing is clear, we don't know exactly how God created. We get an idea from His Word that He can create something from nothing, but that is a concept we, with our limited human comprehension, cannot understand.

As I mentioned earlier, it really does no good to argue inconsistencies because there will always be an argument against an argument. By the time this book is published, new information will have come to light on either side, thus seemingly nullifying each other. We can all rationalize our thinking, especially when vague, presumed variables are part of the equation. But with that said, I find all this fascinating. We should question everything, even science, especially if it is a hypothesis taught as fact. I am in no way a scientist; I am just a person who loves to read about science. What follows are some questions to ponder concerning the validity of radiometric dating that arose in my mind as I studied this subject:

Were the beginning conditions of our planet known? We can't be sure the variables involved with radiometric dating involve a closed system. For instance, has the earth's magnetic field remained constant since the beginning? If it was stronger at one time, that would mean less cosmic rays and less carbon–14 would exist, resulting in an inaccurate reading of any radiocarbon dating done to an object from a time when carbon–14 presence was less.

How do we know what the ratio of carbon–12 to carbon–14 was in an organic substance to begin with?

Has our atmospheric composition been constant since the beginning? An in-depth study of Genesis and the era before the flood suggests that the atmosphere was indeed much thicker and more like a water canopy (Gen. 1:6–8). Scientists have studied air bubbles trapped in amber fossils, and they have found that the air in the bubbles is richer in oxygen, some almost by 50 percent, suggesting our atmosphere was indeed much different in the past. If it was thicker at one time, less cosmic rays would have reached the earth, and the amount of carbon–14 would be less.

Was the beginning daughter to parent isotope ratio known? How do we know when rocks were first forged, and that the clock, from which scientists are measuring, was set to zero? This presents a problem. Isochrons are the proposed answer to this problem, but it also rests on several assumptions.

Could there be contamination or additional daughter or parent isotopes? This is a question we can't always answer.

The Big Bang Theory

The fact that this planet has not been completely destroyed by our own hands of greediness and selfishness is the result of God holding back the four winds of strife mentioned in Revelation 7:1. He is intervening, not allowing us to fully reap what we sow in destroying this earth or our own bodies. Many think the seven last plagues mentioned in Revelation will strictly be a result of God's wrath, but I believe they will be the result of God ceasing to intervene in saving us from our own self-destructiveness. This world was completely different before the flood; it was perfect in every way, poetry and beauty beyond what could be imagined. What we see now is a shadow of what once was and what will be again when we have the privilege of beholding Jesus re-creating the new earth after this great controversy is finally finished.

The universe is superbly master-minded to sustain life. Everywhere we look we can see evidence of a designer who holds all the checks and balances in place.

Even though this earth exists as a dim reflection of what it once was, there still exists beauty in certain parts of the world that remind us of what we were made to behold. From the island of Kauai, to the Great Barrier Reef, to the Swiss Alps, to the tiny Ruby-Throated Hummingbird, to the zebra, and way beyond to the Ring Nebula 2,283 light years away, all are proof of the creative artistry of Elohim. We were created with five main senses—touch, taste, sight, hearing, and smell—that proves to me that the natural world was created for our pleasure and enjoyment. The taste of a sweet watermelon, the smell of cottonwood trees, the sound of your favorite song, the touch of your loved one in the form of a kiss on the cheek, or the beauty of beholding a rainbow at sunset over the Grand Canyon—these were all created for our enjoyment; they are gifts from God to us. But the thought of this world being created for our senses to enjoy goes beyond the obvious to the scientific.

Consider the anthropic principle. If any one fundamental physical constant was minutely different, we would not be here to debate intelligent design. For example a neutron is .1 percent heavier than a proton. If this mass ratio were slightly different, even just .1 percent heavier, life as we know it would not exist because all protons would be neutrons. The universe is superbly master-minded to sustain life. Everywhere we look we can see evidence of a designer who holds all the checks and balances in place.

There are many inconsistencies in the Big Bang Theory that have created many questions and demand many hypotheses to account for observations such as:

> Dark matter: Attempts to explain the existence of galaxy clusters and grouping and the galactic rotation curve problem.
> Dark energy: Attempts to explain accelerating distant supernovae.
> Nucleosynthesis Theory: Attempts to explain why the temperature of the universe is colder than expected.

Why are mature galaxies seen in the "early" universe? Why don't quasars follow Hubble's law? These and many other important questions that might validate the Big Bang Theory remain unanswered, at least at the time of writing this book.

The Big Bang theory falls short many times in the attempt to produce predictions that agree with observations. Almost 95 percent of the universe is said to be made of an abstruse substance called dark matter that we cannot, and have not ever seen. An unseen glue that holds our universe together and keeps harmonious order? Sounds like faith must be involved in this theory, just as all theories must involve some form of faith.

"You Will Not Surely Die"–Satan's Lie in the Garden of Eden

Is the human soul, body, and spirit separate and distinct? Is the soul immortal? And could a God who is said to be the very definition of love, torment people for eternity?

Before I tackle this enormously complex topic, I have to say, because this way of thinking is so grafted into our mental fibers, I found it extremely exhausting to study these concepts. The ability to recognize the subtle deceptions laid out in our philosophies, which have been passed down from Greek philosophers and beyond, and the ability to study and distinguish texts taken out of context in the Bible to support these philosophies, takes an incredible amount of time. I prayed for discernment to be able to recognize the subtle and crafty, slightly false nuances that have over centuries culminated themselves into the gross deceptions we have today. It has been more difficult to study and write a clear, concise and understandable flow of this deceptive topic than any other subject I've ever written about.

God has had to turn my understanding upside down about what I thought were basic premises about my existence now and in the future. Everywhere we look, in movies and the news, in churches, and in eastern philosophies, we are taught one thing over and over, when in fact the Bible tells us another. I pray God will write through me to you, the reader, because I cannot on my own shed full light on this deception and how it affects our perception of our self-worth, Jesus' love, and everything else in our lives.

The theological philosophy, our soul is immortal and can exist separate and distinct from our bodies, has woven itself into mainstream and Christian ways of thinking. It may seem to be an almost insignificant detail, but this subtle pagan theory leads to many major deceptive ways of thinking, contributing to gross misrepresentations of God's character, one of which is the belief, because our soul's are immortal, that there exists an eternal, tormenting, burning hell.

Many biblical deceptions exist because Bible texts are taken out of context, meaning there might be 101 verses referring to a topic, but only a few of those 101 verses at first glance seemingly contradict what the other 98 say. People have taken many of these out of context verses and ran with them, creating a plethora of theories and philosophies concerning many of life's most important questions. This is exactly what has happened with these theories, pagan philosophies, and deceptions. The first deception—that we are immortal, which Satan used to trick Eve—is being combined with these out of context verses and is being accepted today as fact in the minds and hearts of a vast majority of individuals.

I appeal to your logical Christian and biblical mind with the following questions that should be asked by every Christian.

Is God a liar? The number one problem with this theory is that if we believe our souls are immortal then we believe God is a liar. YHVH, in the Garden of Eden, told Adam and Eve if they ate from the tree of the knowledge of good and evil that they would surely die, but the serpent, when talking to Eve, told her she would *not* surely die. The belief that there is an eternal burning hell where those who are punished go is the belief that we have an immortal soul, being alive in hell, tortured forever, is not death, it is eternal life in misery. And of course, this philosophy of an eternal burning hell also goes against the fact that God is love, and that it is impossible for God to lie. (See Titus 1:2, KJV.)

The lie that Satan told Eve in the Garden of Eden has been perpetuated since the beginning of time. Each generation that has lived since Adam and Eve has taken a part of this immortal soul concept to different levels. Eastern philosophies teach versions of this concept of getting rid of our bodies and time and matter and existing in a plane of existence as a spirit, reaching a higher plain of consciousness. The Greek philosophers profoundly influenced upon society certain aspects of this philosophy. They believed that time and matter were bad and corruptible, our bodies got old and feeble and kept us from reaching our full potential in most every way, so they, not knowing the Bible and the truth about sin, thought, if we could get rid of our corruptible bodies, we will be able to reach the pinnacle of our existence.

Many Christians and eastern philosophies take on this idea that our physical bodies are what make us corruptible and that if we could be detached from our physical bodies, we would be free to reach our full potentials or somewhat of a nirvana state. But God, before the entrance of sin, said everything He made was good, yes very good, even our bodies. It was sin and the separation from God that corrupted the matter of our bodies and ultimately destroyed them, not our bodies and matter itself.

Once we are free from sin and not separated from our life giver, will we be free from death, not when we are free from time and our bodies. Jesus is the life-giver, He is the way the truth and the life.

Is only God innately immortal? If He is as the Bible claims He is, then He is the only one who can bestow immortality. To be permanently separated from His life-giving Holy Spirit is to die. To say our souls are immortal in and of themselves is to give ourselves glory, meaning we aren't recognizing God as the perpetuator, the creator, and sustainer of life. First Timothy 6:16 says only God is immortal. We were not created to be immortal in and of ourselves. We were created to be immortal by staying connected to God physically and mentally and by eating from the tree of life.

"Later, the Lord God said, 'Look! The man has become like one of us in knowing good and evil. Now, so he won't reach out, also take from the tree of life, eat, and then live forever—' therefore the Lord God expelled the man from the garden of Eden so he would work the ground from which he had been taken. After he had expelled the man, the Lord God placed winged angels at the eastern end of the garden of Eden, along with a fiery, turning sword, to prevent access to the tree of life" (Gen. 3:22–24, ISV). This verse seems to indicate a continual eating of the fruit from the tree of life was required to have immortality.

If we were created having immortal souls, why would we need Jesus to save us from death? Why would His first coming be necessary? If we could live forever no matter what, why did Jesus have to die to destroy death and the grave as the Bible tells us? There would be no reason to destroy death because death, according to this philosophy, doesn't exist, right? And this also diminishes Jesus' sacrifice in death for us. Because if His soul didn't really die, and He wasn't body, spirit, and soul in the grave (which are not independent of one another), how is that really death and how would that be defeating death? The Bible is very clear that Jesus had not ascended to His Father until after His resurrection (see John 20:17). Satan's first deception in the Garden of Eden, "you will not surely die," led to the beginning of this sin problem for the human race, and it has morphed into every imaginable deception the devil, his angels, and our dark minds could think up. Where is the love of Jesus in any of this thinking? No wonder there exists so many who refuse to know God.

If our souls go to heaven when we die, why is there such an enormous emphasis in the New and Old Testament about the second coming of Jesus? Jesus Himself spoke quite a bit about His returning to save the elect who would be living and to resurrect those who were dead in Christ back to life to be brought to heaven. Why would there need to be a resurrection at all if everyone was already in heaven? Some say the resurrection will be for the souls in heaven to come and be united with their new bodies, but this doesn't make any sense either because the overwhelming majority of verses in the Bible pertaining to the second coming of Jesus suggest that when we see Him coming a second time it will be the first time we've ever actually seen Him, that our faith will finally be sight. If we've spent years up in heaven with Jesus and the angels before the second coming, how will this be the first time our faith will be made sight?

The majority of texts in the Bible teach us that the soul does not go anywhere at the time of death and that the body, spirit, and soul are not independent of one another. When the body dies, the breath or spirit that Jesus breathed into us to make us into a living soul returns to God, and our bodies return to the dust from which we were formed in the beginning. This is working in opposite to the equation of life, which YHVH used to create us in the beginning. Genesis 2:7 says, "And the Lord God formed man of the dust of the ground, and breathed into his nostrils the breath of life; and man became a living soul" (KJV).

The following are verses relating to what happens when we die and also to the second coming of Jesus:

> For to him that is joined to all the living there is hope: for a living dog is better than a dead lion. For the living know that they shall die: but the dead know not any thing, neither have they any more a reward; for the memory of them is forgotten.

Also their love, and their hatred, and their envy, is now perished; neither have they any more a portion for ever in any
thing that is done under the sun. (Eccles. 9:4–6, KJV)

When the silver cord is severed, the golden vessel is broken, the
pitcher is shattered at the fountain, and the wheel is broken at
the cistern, then man's dust will go back to the earth, returning
to what it was, and the spirit will return to the God who gave
it. (Eccles. 12:6, 7, ISV)

For this we say to you by the word of the Lord, that we who
are alive *and* remain until the coming of the Lord will by no
means precede those who are asleep. For the Lord Himself will
descend from heaven with a shout, with the voice of an archan-
gel, and with the trumpet of God. And the dead in Christ will
rise first. Then we who are alive *and* remain shall be caught up
together with them in the clouds to meet the Lord in the air.
And thus we shall always be with the Lord. Therefore comfort
one another with these words. (1 Thess. 4:15–18, NKJV)

How could we know nothing if we are living spirits without bodies existing
in heaven or hell? Why would the dead in Christ need to rise if they are alive
in heaven, and why would there be a blessed hope of His second coming if
when we die our souls are already with Him? As I mentioned, many times it
seems as though these verses are suggesting we will be meeting Christ for the
first time in person, physically seeing Him for the first time, but how can that
be if we are already alive as spirits in heaven hanging out with Him?

"But if the Spirit of Him who raised Jesus from the dead dwells in you,
He who raised Christ from the dead will also give life to your mortal bodies
through His Spirit who dwells in you" (Rom. 8:11, NKJV).

Our hope isn't in looking forward to living as spirits without bodies, our
hope is in having new bodies that exist without the scars of sin and its result
of decay and death.

"Very truly I tell you, whoever hears my word and believes him who sent me has eternal life and will not be judged but has crossed over from death to life. Very truly I tell you, a time is coming and has now come when the dead will hear the voice of the Son of God and those who hear will live. For as the Father has life in himself, so he has granted the Son also to have life in himself. And he has given him authority to judge because he is the Son of Man" (John 5:24–27, NIV).

"Men *and* brethren, let *me* speak freely to you of the patriarch David, that he is *both dead and buried, and his tomb is with us to this day.* Therefore, being a prophet, and knowing that God had sworn with an oath to him that of the fruit of his body, according to the flesh, He would raise up the Christ to sit on his throne, he, foreseeing this, spoke concerning the resurrection of the Christ, that His soul was not left in Hades, nor did His flesh see corruption. This Jesus God has raised up, of which we are all witnesses. Therefore being exalted to the right hand of God, and having received from the Father the promise of the Holy Spirit, He poured out this which you now see and hear. *For David did not ascend into the heavens,* but he says himself: 'The Lord said to my Lord, "Sit at My right hand, till I make Your enemies Your footstool"'" (Acts 2:29–35, NKJV, italics supplied).

One should ask, after considering this verse, if David died and is in heaven, why is Paul saying here that David is in the grave, dead and buried, where he is awaiting the resurrection. First Corinthians 15:42–55 says:

So also *is* the resurrection of the dead. *The body* is sown in corruption, it is raised in incorruption. It is sown in dishonor, it is raised in glory. It is sown in weakness, it is raised in power. It is sown a natural body, it is raised a spiritual body. There is a natural body, and there is a spiritual body. And so it is written, "The first man Adam became a living being." The last Adam *became* a life-giving spirit.

However, the spiritual is not first, but the natural, and afterward the spiritual. The first man *was* of the earth, *made* of dust; the second Man *is* the Lord from heaven. As *was* the *man* of dust, so also *are* those *who are made* of dust; and as *is* the heavenly *Man,* so also *are* those *who are* heavenly. And as we have borne the image of the *man* of dust, we shall also bear the image of the heavenly Man.

Now this I say, brethren, that flesh and blood cannot inherit the kingdom of God; nor does corruption inherit incorruption. Behold, I tell you a mystery: We shall not all sleep, but we shall all be changed—in a moment, in the twinkling of an eye, at the last trumpet. For the trumpet will sound, and the dead will be raised incorruptible, and we shall be changed. For this corruptible must put on incorruption, and this mortal *must* put on immortality. So when this corruptible has put on incorruption, and this mortal has put on immortality, then shall be brought to pass the saying that is written: "Death is swallowed up in victory. O Death, where *is* your sting? O Hades, where *is* your victory?" (NKJV)

Notice here how Paul says the dead will be raised with a spiritual body, not a spirit without a body. Also Jesus (or the last Adam), Paul says, became a life-giving spirit, which means Jesus brought life to humanity and conquered death. Jesus is being contrasted with the first Adam who was created a living being but became corrupted and brought death to humanity. We know Jesus had a physical body because He told Thomas to touch Him in John 20:27 and Jesus ate with the disciples after His resurrection. And we will have bodies like Jesus' glorious body as it says in Philippians 3:20, 21 "For our conversation is in heaven; from whence also we look for the Saviour, the Lord Jesus Christ: Who shall change our vile body, that it may be fashioned like unto his glorious body, according to the working whereby he is able even to subdue all things unto himself" (KJV).

Jesus is not spirit, He is physical, and we will be a physical body, not a spirit without a physical body. Many people read Scripture with preconceived notions from what they've been taught throughout their lives. In other verses when Paul talks about the flesh, it is similar to what he is saying in the verses above, our bodies now, which are corruptible because of the disease of sin, is the flesh or temporary tent. Our new bodies after translation when Jesus comes again will be free of the effects of sin and corruption, perfect in every way, but not without form as a spirit.

Second Corinthians 5:1–5 says, "For we know that if our earthly house, *this* tent [our bodies that can decay because of sin], is destroyed, we have a building from God, a house not made with hands, eternal in the heavens. For in this we groan, earnestly desiring to be clothed with our habitation which is from heaven, if indeed, having been clothed, we shall not be found naked.

For we who are in *this* tent groan, being burdened, not because we want to be unclothed, but further clothed, that mortality may be swallowed up by life. Now He who has prepared us for this very thing *is* God, who also has given us the Spirit as a guarantee" (NKJV).

What Paul means here is that Jesus has promised us an immortal body, which we are waiting for; we are not waiting to be free floating spirits. God created us with bodies to enjoy the pleasure of our senses with which He created us; He did not create us just to be a spirit. He does not want us to go to heaven and not be able to touch the grass and feel the sea of glass, or to smell a never fading flower, or to taste the luscious fruit of the tree of life. He wants us to be able to feel His arms around us when He gives us a hug and holds us to His chest.

On several occasions, approximately fifty, the Bible compares death to sleep (see Dan. 12:2). If we go straight to heaven or hell when we die, how can we be sleeping in the dust and then awakening at a later point? We learn in Revelation 20 that there is a second death after the 1,000 years. So if there is a second death, there must be a first death. This first death is what is being referred to as sleep in the Bible. It's referred to as sleep because the first death is not final, the dead in Christ will be raised to life at the first resurrection as we saw in 1 Thessalonians, and the dead in Satan will be raised again in the second resurrection (inferred here because it mentions the first resurrection and second death) after the 1,000 years.

I saw thrones on which were seated those who had been given authority to judge. And I saw the souls of those who had been beheaded because of their testimony about Jesus and because of the word of God. They had not worshiped the beast or its image and had not received its mark on their foreheads or their hands. They came to life and reigned with Christ a thousand years. (The rest of the dead did not come to life until the thousand years were ended.) This is the first resurrection. Blessed and holy are those who share in the first resurrection. The second death has no power over them, but they will be priests of God and of Christ and will reign with him for a thousand years. (Rev. 20:4–6, NIV)

So it is like a sleep in the sense that there will be a point at which people will awaken again—it is temporary. It is clear that, just like when you are sleeping, there is no consciousness, for King Solomon said in Ecclesiastes that the dead know nothing. The following Bible passages also support this notion.

"Why did I not perish at birth, and die as I came from the womb? Why were there knees to receive me and breasts that I might be nursed? For now I would be lying down in peace; I would be asleep and at rest." (Job 3:11–13, NIV)

These things He said, and after that He said to them, "Our friend Lazarus sleeps, but I go that I may wake him up." Then His disciples said, "Lord, if he sleeps he will get well." However, Jesus spoke of his death, but they thought that He was speaking about taking rest in sleep. Then Jesus said to them plainly, "Lazarus is dead." (John 11:11–14, NKJV)

Now when He had said these things, He cried with a loud voice, "Lazarus, come forth!" And he who had died came out bound hand and foot with graveclothes, and his face was wrapped with a cloth. Jesus said to them, "Loose him, and let him go." (John 11:43, 44, NKJV)

If Lazarus' soul was alive in heaven as many Christians believe, then why did Jesus call him forth from the tomb and not down from heaven? Lazarus was neither in heaven or hell, he was asleep or dead in the tomb.

And after six days Jesus taketh Peter, James, and John his brother, and bringeth them up into an high mountain apart, and was transfigured before them: and his face did shine as the sun, and his raiment was white as the light. And, behold, there appeared unto them Moses and Elias talking with him. Then answered Peter, and said unto Jesus, Lord, it is good for us to be here: if thou wilt, let us make here three tabernacles; one for thee, and one for Moses, and one for Elias. (Matt. 17:1–4, KJV)

There are a couple points to notice in this Matthew text. First of all, this scripture says Jesus was transfigured, or He was given a new form, a glorious, incorruptible body at this moment, showing the disciples the translated body of Jesus and the incorruptible translated bodies of Moses and Elijah. This was to give them faith in Jesus as the Messiah and to show them what they had to look forward to at the second coming when everyone will be changed in the twinkling of an eye. On the Mount of Transfiguration Jesus, Moses, and Elijah all appeared in bodily form; they weren't free floating spirits. As I said before, many Christians believe that when we die our souls and spirits go to heaven. They state that when Jesus returns the second time we'll get an incorruptible physical body to which our spirits will be joined. If that's true, how come Moses, who had died before he was taken to heaven, appeared in bodily form? The second coming hadn't occurred yet for him to get his new body.

Since Abel's death, which was the first recorded human death, those who have died are sleeping in the grave as we have read in previous verses. However, there are some people God has chosen to take to heaven. We know of Enoch, Elijah, and Moses because the Bible tells us their story. Moses died and was then raised to life and taken to heaven. This gives hope to those who have died that there will indeed be a resurrection. Enoch and Elijah were brought to heaven without experiencing death. This gives hope to those who will be alive at the time of Jesus' second coming.

What is the recipe for life? Genesis 2:7 says that "God formed [or molded] man of the dust [or clay] of the ground, and breathed into his nostrils the breath [or spirit] of life; and man became a living soul" (KJV). So body + spirit = living soul. We have learned that the body is the physical vessel, flesh or tent as Paul calls it. The spirit or breath, according to Job 33:4, seems to be interchangeable. And soul is the living entity, or the person as a whole of body and spirit. The Bible, in Genesis 12:5 and Genesis 14:21, interchanges the words soul and person because the soul is the living entity. The immortality of the soul being able to exist separate from the body is assumed and added to certain questionable texts by people who hold the subconscious teachings of the Greek philosophers. God-fearing Hebrews originally did not believe the soul was separate from the body.

The word spirit is interchangeable with breath in the Bible. We need to have respiration to live. We need to breath in oxygen, which is carried from our lungs by our red blood cells and dispersed to every part of our physical body, in order to remain living. Our need of oxygen correlates to our need of the living power of the Holy Spirit in our lives. If a living thing is completely cut off from God or the Holy Spirit, it dies. God the Holy Spirit gives life; He continually breathes or imparts life into us through the perfect functioning of our respiratory and circulatory system.

Think about this. The Holy Spirit brought life to the incarnate Jesus in Mary's womb: "The angel answered, 'The Holy Spirit will come on you, and the power of the Most High will overshadow you. So the holy one to be born will be called the Son of God'" (Luke 1:35, NIV). At the end of the book of John in chapter 20, verse 22, Jesus breathed on His disciples and said, "Receive the Holy Spirit" (NIV). Jesus is YHVH, the Creator who originally breathed into our nostrils the breath of life, thus making us into a living soul. The same breath Jesus breathed on His disciples to receive the Holy Spirit was the same breath He breathed into Adam and Eve. There's depth there in that connection that I haven't fully comprehended yet, but I find it beautiful nonetheless.

Our breath, also called spirit, is evidence of the presence of the Holy Spirit in us, sustaining our lives: "Do you not know that your bodies are temples of the Holy Spirit, who is in you, whom you have received from God? You are not your own; you were bought at a price. Therefore honor God with your bodies" (1 Cor. 6:19, 20, NIV).

Whether a person is for God or against God, everyone receives the gift of life and is given the choice to choose life or death. Matthew 5:45 reminds us of this principle: "He causes his sun to rise on the evil and the good, and sends rain on the righteous and the unrighteous" (NIV). He wants everyone to be saved in His kingdom, and He shows every person love beyond what any of us deserve.

It's also important to notice in Genesis 2:7 that Adam *became* a living soul, He did not have a living soul. There are about 1,650 mentions of soul and spirit in the Bible and none of them seem to indicate the soul is immortal.

With all that said, there are a few texts that appear to contradict all I just wrote. Those verses being, for instance, 2 Corinthians 5:8, Philippians 1:23, Luke 16:19–31, Luke 23:43, and 1 Samuel 28. The texts written by Paul in 2 Corinthians and Philippians are not talking about death and a soulless body or a spirit going straight to heaven; he is talking about the desire to be with God in heaven one day. He does not say he would instantaneously see Jesus upon tasting death because this would conflict with many of the other verses I mentioned earlier pertaining to Jesus' second coming.

Paul says in verse 6 of 2 Corinthians 5, while we are at home in the body, we are absent from Christ. In no way is he saying only when we become a free-floating spirit that we can be with Christ immediately upon death. He is saying here that as long as we are in our earthly, sin-marred bodies we are separated from Christ. It is when He returns and gives us new, translated bodies that are not earthly and are not subject to the decay of sin, as Paul mentions in several other texts, that we will be united with Christ for eternity. That is what he means in these texts.

In Philippians 1:23 Paul says he is betwixt between the thought of dying and being with Christ or living and being here for the believers at that time. It is not saying that upon dying he will immediately go to heaven; that is inferred. It would contradict most every other verse he's written about this subject. To not contradict the other Bible verses about this subject, he must mean that if he died the next thing he would be aware of was Jesus resurrecting him.

Perhaps the most confusing texts on this subject are the two I listed in Luke. Luke 23:43 is the passage where Jesus tells the thief on the cross he will be with Jesus in heaven. "And Jesus said unto him, Verily I say unto thee, today shalt thou be with me in paradise" (KJV). This sounds as though Jesus is saying that today the thief would be going to heaven. In the original Greek text, there was no comma after thee. When translated, the comma was added after thee. Look how different the text would read if we changed the placing of the comma, "And Jesus said unto him, Verily I say unto thee today, shalt thou be with me in paradise." So, was Jesus telling the thief he'd be in heaven that day, or was he simply saying I'm telling you at this moment in time that you will be with Me in heaven at the resurrection. I believe it is the latter explanation because it's the one that does not contradict the majority of Bible verses on this subject.

The other story in Scripture that trips people up on this subject is the parable of the rich man and Lazarus found in Luke 16. This is perhaps the largest passage that people use to prove the theory that our souls and bodies are separate, that when we die we go to heaven or hell, and that there is an eternal hell. First of all, this parable was a story that was told within the Jewish culture of Jesus' time, which is most likely the reason for the use of specific names. To many Jews, being a rich, wealthy, healthy Jew meant you were in good standing with God and that God looked upon those in this category with favor on this earth and in the new earth.

If you look at this story in context within the book of Luke as a whole, you begin to see a connection with the other parables told and Jesus' actions, which all point toward what He was trying to teach. Luke 16 opens with another parable told of a rich man and talks of the responsibility we should have with money, illustrating the point that the love of money is idolatry and you cannot serve two masters, God and money. He wasn't teaching that money is evil; He was teaching that the love of money is evil. He was also in effect teaching that if we use our money wisely and also use it to help others and further the kingdom of God it shows we are faithful to God and can be trusted with additional gifts from Him. It also shows we are storing our treasures in heaven and not living in faithlessness of the instant gratification of the here and now.

Right before the parable of Lazarus and the rich man, in verse 14, it is written that the Pharisees were lovers of money and thought themselves to be just and upright. Although many of them were wealthy and educated and part of high society, their status didn't mean they were favored by God. Their pompous and pious ways showed they were lovers of themselves and not God. In the Lazarus parable, which begins in verse 19, God uses their own cultural parable to show them the truth of their nature and their future reward if they continue to live a life of selfishness.

At the end of the Lazarus parable, Jesus does something incredibly profound, He prophesies about the resurrection of His friend Lazarus, who not coincidentally has the same name, and the effect it will have on them, which is none. Even after the miraculous resurrection of Lazarus, the Pharisees still refused to believe in Jesus. "He said to him, If they do not hear *and* listen to Moses and the Prophets, neither will they be persuaded *and* convinced *and* believe [even] if someone should rise from the dead" (Luke 16:31, AMP). He was in effect telling them their hearts were so hard and they were such lovers of the lies that eased their consciences that no prophet, not even God in the flesh, and no person, not even a person who was raised from the dead, could convince them of the truth of Jesus Christ and His salvation.

Not long after Jesus told the Lazarus parable and before Jesus' crucifixion, He raised His friend Lazarus to life after days of being dead in the tomb. This act was the crowing proclamation and proof that Jesus was the true Messiah for whom the Jews had been waiting; unfortunately, the religious leaders were unreceptive because His power threatened their power. I assure you, Jesus would not contradict His own teachings and the rest of the Bible's teachings about the nature of death and body and soul and spirit. The story of the rich man and Lazarus was a parable used to speak to the hearts of the rabbis on a familiar level they could grasp.

The last seemingly complicated text I'd like to address is in 1 Samuel 28. In this chapter we read the story of Saul visiting the witch of Endor who calls the prophet Samuel from the dead so that Saul can ask him about the outcome of the impending war with the Philistines. It's important to note here in verse 14 that the Bible says Saul perceived it was Samuel. The text does not say it was in reality the actual prophet Samuel. Another important factor to consider here is found in verse 9, where we read that Saul was engaging in a forbidden act (see Deut. 18:11; Lev. 19:31; 20:27). It was unlawful for a person to speak to the dead or to a person who speaks to the dead.

Considering these facts, it cannot have really been Samuel, but an angel of Satan who was actually speaking to Saul. The righteous souls who are supposedly in heaven now would not be able to sneak out from under God's watchful eye and come down here to earth to violate one of His laws. There is no way, if they were righteous, that they would want to violate God's law. Some may note the fact that Satan's angel, who had disguised himself as the deceased prophet Samuel, predicted Saul's impending death. This does not mean the spirit was Samuel; it just means the angel was able to predict, based on common sense of the study of cause and effect, the outcome of the battle. Throughout history humans, who are lesser in mental capacity than an angel, have correctly predicted outcomes, whether from common sense or divine intervention. It is not illogical that a fallen angel disguised as the prophet Samuel could predict an outcome. Also, God may have allowed the fallen angel to know the future so that Saul would know his fate.

So, the million-dollar question remains: why do people see dead loved ones like the boy in the movie *Heaven Is for Real*? Or how is it some people report that there are ghosts and hauntings of places or homes by spirits? The only possible logical explanation when considering the truths of the Bible as a whole is that what these people are actually seeing are Satan's angels masquerading as others who have died. We know Satan interacts with whomever he can deceive. Jesus said Satan is the prince of this world and that He will try to deceive us in any way possible. John tells us, "Dear friends, do not believe every spirit, but test the spirits to see whether they are from God, because many false prophets have gone out into the world. This is how you can recognize the Spirit of God: Every spirit that acknowledges that Jesus Christ has come in the flesh is from God, but every spirit that does not acknowledge Jesus is not from God. This is the spirit of the antichrist, which you have heard is coming and even now is already in the world" (1 John 4:1–3, NIV).

I have known a few people and heard of many others who have been harassed or even "nicely" visited by spirits, some who are disguised as those who have died. Satan will attempt to deceive in whatever way possible to distort the image of God and lead people down the wrong path. "Enter through the narrow gate. For wide is the gate and broad is the road that leads to destruction, and many enter through it" (Matt. 7:13, NIV). If one is not grounded in the truth of the Bible, it is so easy for Satan to manipulate and get people to believe and do as he pleases by sending a supposed loved one to tell them what he wants them to do. Who's going to deny their deceased grandmother's wishes if they didn't know better?

Unfortunately, this deception has vast ramifications and has created a domino effect and a web of lies that makes it easy for Satan to manipulate and distort the character of God. Hopefully through this study you understand that the Bible teaches that the body, soul, and spirit are not independent of one another. When a person dies they know nothing, their bodies decay in the grave, and their spirit returns to God from which it came until the resurrection at Jesus' second coming.

The idea of an eternal burning hell is completely contrary to every description of the character of God.

There are many other deceptions that stem from this false philosophy, but the one that causes more indifference to God above all is the idea that there is an eternal burning hell. The idea of an eternal burning hell is completely contrary to every description of the character of God. Hell does exist, the

Bible is clear about that, but hell is not what popular Christianity makes it out to be.

Wherever the Bible mentions the terms forever, everlasting, or eternal, it is in the context of either being a large amount of time for which one cannot see the end, or a result that is indefinite, or that there is a memory of that event that has lasted or will last a very long time or indefinitely. Looking at the Bible as a whole, no where is it taught that the wicked will be kept alive to be tortured for a never-ending, indefinite amount of time. This is a complete falsehood and a blasphemy against the name and character of God. The following are some verses pertaining to the definition of the aforementioned adjectives.

And the streams thereof shall be turned into pitch, and the dust thereof into brimstone, and the land thereof shall become burning pitch. It shall not be quenched night nor day; the smoke thereof shall go up for ever: from generation to generation it shall lie waste; none shall pass through it for ever and ever. (Isa. 34:9, 10, KJV)

Obviously Edom is not still burning, nor is there still smoke rising from it. But the destruction and desolation of that city exists to this day. It's not the eternal act of being punished; it's the eternal result of the punishment.

Even as Sodom and Gomorrha, and the cities about them in like manner, giving themselves over to fornication, and going after strange flesh, are set forth for an example, suffering the vengeance of eternal fire. (Jude 1:7, KJV)

Sodom and Gomorrah were destroyed by fire and brimstone raining down from the sky. They were completely incinerated, and nothing exists where these cities once were. In Genesis, Moses described the valleys there as lush and fertile, but now that entire area is a giant wasteland and there is not a burning fire there today; however, the desolation still exists which was the result from the destruction of those cities.

But if ye will not hearken unto me to hallow the sabbath day, and not to bear a burden, even entering in at the gates of Jerusalem on the sabbath day; then will I kindle a fire in the gates thereof, and it shall devour the palaces of Jerusalem, and it shall not be quenched. (Jer. 17:27, KJV)

The Bible mentions unquenchable fires a few times, but there are obviously not fires still burning from hundreds or thousands of years ago. When the Bible mentions unquenchable, it is saying the fire could not be put out. It had to run its course and consume all that was in its path until there was nothing left to feed it. We still say things like this today when referring to fires that are just too powerful to put out. But eventually they do go out once what is fueling them is consumed.

Then his master shall bring him unto the judges; he shall also bring him to the door, or unto the door post; and his master shall bore his ear through with an aul; and he shall serve him for ever. (Exod. 21:6, KJV)

Obviously a person cannot be a slave to someone else forever, for they will eventually die. This is another example of how forever is used to express a long period of time of which we don't know the end, such as the length of someone's life.

In 2 Thessalonians 1:6–9 we are giving the definition of hell:

Seeing it is a righteous thing with God to recompense tribulation to them that trouble you; And to you who are troubled rest with us, when the Lord Jesus shall be revealed from heaven with his mighty angels, In flaming fire taking vengeance on them that know not God, and that obey not the gospel of our Lord Jesus Christ: Who shall be punished with everlasting destruction from the presence of the Lord, and from the glory of his power. (KJV)

The eternal, everlasting, or forever destruction is the result of being permanently cut off from the presence of God and His glory and power, which sustains life. And this permanent cutting off is not God's choice; it is our choice. We can choose to accept life and Jesus as our gift and representative, or we can choose to believe Satan and his lies concerning God's intentions for us and continue in rebellion against His laws and life of love. Only those who truly know God and reflect His character of love will be able to stand in His presence, which is a consuming fire.

Those who live their lives in relationship with God, who know Him as a personal friend, will be able to enjoy living in the presence of God. The wicked who don't know God will cry out for the rocks to fall on them to hide them from the presence of God. In God's mercy, because they would not be happy existing in the constant presence of God, those who have been given ample opportunity to know Him and have chosen to disregard His free gift of salvation will be consumed. They will be as if they never existed.

In Revelation 21 we are told Jesus will wipe away every tear from our eyes and that there will be no more tears, death, sorrow, crying, or pain. If this is true, how can there be an eternal burning hell? There is no way Jesus, the angels, or anyone else could possibly enjoy heaven and eternal life if people are being eternally tormented—paradise in heaven would be impossible. "For I take no pleasure in the death of anyone, declares the Sovereign Lord. Repent and live!" (Ezek. 18:32, NIV). God wishes for all to have eternal life, so when those who have made their final decision choose not to be with God, there will exist a certain emptiness in His heart for the eternal absence of the fallen angels and humans. Jesus tells us He will comfort us and dry our eyes, that tears will be no more, but have you ever wondered who will comfort Him in this somber hour when time closes?

The soul, body, and spirit are inseparable, and when we die, we wait in the grave until we are resurrected. We know nothing until that point when Jesus brings us back to life. The Bible does not teach that there will be an eternal burning hell where people will be tormented for eternity, never to die. These philosophies are completely contradictory to the Bible and the love of God.

Are the Ten Commandments Done Away With?

In opposition to the doctrine of eternal hell and the fear that that produces, people have adopted the notion of once saved always saved, basically creating a system of automatic entrance into heaven.

One of the issues with this philosophy is that those who accepted Jesus and then walked away would be miserable in the presence of God forever if He saved them while still living in rebellion. The Bible talks a lot about repenting of our sins and turning to God so that we will be saved. If we were automatically saved, why would we need to repent and stop doing whatever cherished sin we've been doing?

"And they shall bring the glory and the honor of the nations into it. But there shall by no means enter it anything that defiles, or causes an abomination or a lie, but only those who are written in the Lamb's Book of Life" (Rev. 21:26, 27, NKJV).

Another theory that goes hand in hand with the once saved always saved mentality is the belief that not only Moses' law, but God's law (the Ten Commandments) were done away with when Jesus died on the cross.

Somehow our understanding of the commandments of God has become confused. We have people on one side who completely disregard them, and we have people on the other side who hold the polar opposite view that we must obey every commandment to be saved. Both sides of this view are wrong. It amazes me how clever Satan is with his subtle mind twisting deceptions.

Before I begin addressing this topic, I must interject that the original Hebrew description of the Ten Commandments were ten suggestions of how we would act if we love Him. They were not commandments per se. Also, most people leave out the introduction to the commandments in Exodus 20. God begins with the statement, "I *am* the Lord your God, who brought you out of the land of Egypt, out of the house of bondage" (verse 2, NKJV). What God was essentially saying was, I freed you, I gave you your lives back, you have a future now, so hopefully you will see My love for you, and you will love Me back. If you love Me, you will live by these suggestions.

The Ten Commandments, as Paul says in Romans 7:7, act as a reflection; it reflects the character of God and shows us just how opposite of that character we are. If we love God, we see how living a life with Him changes us, and we begin subconsciously following His laws of love: "You will recognize them by their fruits" (Matt. 7:16, ESV). How would we know we need a Savior or how would we know if we were really committing an act against God if we didn't have a guide to show us? If we were pulled over for doing 55 mph in a 35 mph zone, but there was no sign posted for speed, would it be fair to get a ticket? Ignorance isn't necessarily always a defense, but there is most certainly no excuse if the sign is posted.

Unfortunately, we see here again that people are grasping at straws to ease their own consciences, and they take a few texts out of context when compared to the entire Bible. The Bible is very clear and repeats over and over again in the Old and New Testaments that those who live in opposition to the love or laws of God are not friends of God and will not receive eternal life. By choosing to follow Satan, they are choosing to be cut off from God. Paul clearly lists the attributes of cherished sins that will cause people to not inherit eternal life and the attributes of those who live by the law of love who will inherit eternal life (see Gal. 5; 1 Cor. 6).

Jesus Himself in John 14:15 said, "If ye love me, keep my commandments" (KJV). He's speaking here of after His death and His returning to heaven. If the commandments were done away with at the cross, why would He say this?

Paul talks extensively about this topic because the Jews were works orientated. He desperately tried to alter their perception and teach them that they were free from the pressure of attempting to obey all 613 laws of the Torah and the ten commandments of God in order to be saved. Do you see the truth in there compared to the deception? Paul said that no works, no law can be kept perfectly in order to be saved; it is impossible. God knew it was impossible for a fallen human to perfectly keep the law of love, so God became human and kept it for us, reclaiming the race to Himself and saving us from the slavery of Satan.

Like the laws of physics, love is an absolute. The characteristics of what makes up God's love will never change.

It is clear in Colossians 2 and other instances of Paul's writings that the laws of Moses in the Old Testament were done away with after the death of Jesus, because He was the fulfillment of those laws. Most of the Mosaic laws pointed forward to Him. Paul did not say that the Ten Commandments were done away with. In Malachi 3:6, God says, "For I am the Lord, I do not change." Like the laws of physics, love is an absolute. The characteristics of what makes up God's love will never change.

The Ten Commandments are summed up, as Jesus said, in two ways: the first four address love for God and the last six talk about love for our fellow humans. The Ten Commandments show us our true character and our desperate need for Jesus. They present a perfect example of what life can be like when we let Jesus live in us and through us.

Most people don't have a problem with "thou shalt not kill" or "thou shalt not steal" because those commandments affect our own well-being and safety, but people struggle with the first four commandments, the ones concerning our love for God.

The commandment with which we seem to have the most indifference toward is the fourth commandment.

"Remember the Sabbath day, to keep it holy. Six days you shall labor and do all your work, but the seventh day *is* the Sabbath of the Lord your God. *In it* you shall do no work: you, nor your son, nor your daughter, nor your male servant, nor your female servant, nor your cattle, nor your stranger who *is* within your gates. For *in* six days the Lord made the heavens and the earth, the sea, and all that *is* in them, and rested the seventh day. Therefore the Lord blessed the Sabbath day and hallowed it." (Exod. 20:8–11, NKJV)

It is the longest commandment, and it is the only one that begins with the word "remember," which makes it pretty ironic that most people have forgotten it. Interestingly, part of this commandment is quoted in Revelation 14:7, making it a seemingly important, not only in the Old Testament world, but the New Testament and beyond.

Many claim Colossians 2:16, 17 as proof against honoring the Sabbath because Paul says, "So let no one judge you in food or in drink, or regarding a festival or a new moon or sabbaths, which are a shadow of things to come, but the substance is of Christ" (NKJV). But Paul is talking about the ritualistic traditions that were a foretelling of the coming of the Messiah. When he wrote about Sabbaths, he was not referring to the Sabbath day. He was referring to the many Sabbath festivals and traditions. Certain Sabbath days before festivals were of more importance, also they had sabbaticals every seven years, and there were other days, years, and months of importance surrounding cycles of seven such as the jubilee years. There is nothing wrong with observing these, and a study of these cycles gives much insight and understanding of prophecy, but no amount of rituals will save you, which was Paul's whole point. The Sabbath day, set aside by God at the opening of time, was to be a permanent observance, and we are told it will be observed after Jesus returns.

Even attempting to honor the Ten Commandments of God is not enough to save you. When we try to do things ourselves, we are attempting to take care of our own salvation, and we are cutting Jesus out of the picture. The Ten Commandments are what we will live by more and more as our hearts are converted and we fall deeper in love with Jesus. His heart becomes our heart. The first step is to have a closer relationship with Jesus, and then the commandments begin to fall in line. It is not the opposite way around. Attempting to follow the commandments to be closer to Jesus will not result in a successful endeavor.

However, to say that the Ten Commandments are done away with and that it's legalism to still consider them is a mistake. Jesus said in Matthew 7:16 that we would know who people are by their fruit, their actions. We say today that actions speak louder than words. If people live their lives willingly and decidedly contrary to the actions of the commandments, then you will know they are not following God. "Everyone who believes that Jesus is the Christ has become a child of God. And everyone who loves the Father loves his children, too. We know we love God's children if we love God and obey his commandments. Loving God means keeping his commandments, and his commandments are not burdensome" (1 John 5:1–3, NLT).

An important point to mention here is that we all break the commandments of God every day, many unknowingly. It is the cherished sins, the sins we know are wrong and have been convicted of but still blatantly participate in, that are fully accountable sins. None of us will ever be completely perfect or Jesus would never have had to become human, but we are called to not have idols before God, and a cherished sin is an idol, whether it's pornography, which is adultery, or whether we don't honor the Sabbath because it's not convenient or cool, or maybe we are jealous of our friend's Maserati, which is coveting, or maybe we just flat out hate and harbor anger against the people who keep cutting us off on the freeway, or maybe you smoke, or do any number of things that destroy your body, the temple of the Holy Spirit. Whatever the cherished sin is that we know is wrong and choose to participate in, if we do not give it up and ask God for help, continuing to engage in that sin will lead to the destruction of our mind, body, and soul and eventually lead to eternal death. When we truly find Christ and learn of His beauty and He is present in our hearts and minds, all things, no matter the addiction, will pale in comparison to Him. His love sets us free. But we must seek Him in earnest first. Jesus said that all those who seek will find.

Some may ask, "Are each of the Ten Commandments of equal importance? Even the fourth commandment about the seventh-day Sabbath?" Yes, they are all important. If we love Him, we will keep *all* His commandments, even the fourth one.

So how do we keep the fourth commandment? We honor the Sabbath day, which the Bible says is the seventh day of the week. The seventh day, not the first day of the week, is a date with God. It is a specific creation of time set aside to meet with our Creator. Many of the Jewish people had made the Sabbath a day of cumbersome rules, but that is not what it is about. It is true that God said to not work on the Sabbath, that six days were for working, but that was to be a blessing, giving us permission to take the day off and commune with others and God. In Exodus and Deuteronomy we are told to remember the Sabbath and our Creator because He made us and redeemed us. I don't understand why it's so inconvenient for people to take the Sabbath off and just enjoy nature and friends and Jesus.

Much of the Christian world celebrates the Sabbath on Sunday, but God says to honor the Sabbath day, the seventh day of the week, which is Saturday. There is controversy as to who changed Saturday Sabbath to Sunday. Some claim it was Constantine in AD 321, and some claim it was changed hundreds of years earlier. Most people point to two main texts that they say serve as evidence that the disciples changed the day of worship from Saturday to Sunday. Those verses are Acts 20:7—"On the first day of the week we came together to break bread. Paul spoke to the people and, because he intended to leave the next day, kept on talking until midnight" (NIV)—and 1 Corinthians 16:1, 2—"Now about the collection for the Lord's people: Do what I told the Galatian churches to do. On the first day of every week, each one of you should set aside a sum of money in keeping with your income, saving it up, so that when I come no collections will have to be made" (NIV).

There is absolutely no proof in the Bible that the Sabbath was changed to Sunday, and I do not see any proof here that the disciples honored Sunday instead of Saturday. The only thing these texts prove is that the disciples met on Sunday to take care of business and to teach. In fact, they most likely met most days of the week to teach and preach and take care of finances and oversee their ministry. These texts do not prove that the Sabbath was changed from the seventh day of the week to the first. It is only conjecture.

There are several instances in the New Testament that specifically say the disciples honored the Sabbath. Acts 13 specifically mentions Paul preaching and teaching on the Sabbath, and he was invited back the following Sabbath to preach, not the next day, which would have been Sunday. In Mark 6:2 and Luke 4:16, we are told that Jesus kept the Sabbath, which was His custom. Jesus also told His disciples in Matthew 24 to pray that when they must flee the city that their flights would not be on the Sabbath. This was a message to them and to the people living in the last days, so if honoring the Sabbath was done away with after His death and resurrection, why would He tell the disciples and us to pray that our flight is not on Sabbath? It is also interesting to note that Jesus died on Friday, and none of the disciples or women would embalm Him Friday evening or Saturday because they were honoring the Sabbath commandment. It wasn't until Sunday, after the Sabbath had passed, that the women went to embalm Jesus and discovered that He had risen.

People call Sunday the Lord's day because it was the day He rose from the dead, and they believe it should be honored as the Sabbath because of His resurrection. But Sunday is not the Lord's day, the Sabbath is. "Then he said to them, 'The Sabbath was made for man, not man for the Sabbath. So the Son of Man is Lord even of the Sabbath'" (Mark 2:27, 28, NIV). "But the seventh day is the sabbath of the Lord thy God" (Exod. 20:10, KJV). "'If you keep your feet from breaking the Sabbath and from doing as you please on my holy day, if you call the Sabbath a delight and the Lord's holy day honorable, and if you honor it by not going your own way and not doing as you please or speaking idle words, then you will find your joy in the Lord, and I will cause you to ride in triumph on the heights of the land and to feast on the inheritance of your father Jacob.' For the mouth of the Lord has spoken" (Isa. 58:13, 14, NIV). In Revelation 1:10 when John said he was in the Spirit on the Lord's day, did he mean Saturday or Sunday? After researching and looking just at the few texts I've mentioned here, I am completely convicted John means the seventh day Saturday.

A difficult but incredibly important mindset that must be changed is the belief that honoring the Sabbath means you are being legalistic. It is, in fact, quite the opposite. The Sabbath is all about exhibiting faith in a relationship with the God who created us and redeemed us. The Sabbath was the day God ceased from His work and enjoyed His new creation. Humans were created on the sixth day, and that evening and morning were the seventh day, our first day of life. The seventh-day Sabbath is all about focusing on our relationship with our Creator and what He has done for us and what He is going to do for us, contemplating His grace and His awesomeness, because it is all about His faithfulness, not our own. Our faith will become sight—that is what honoring the Sabbath teaches us. It helps us look forward to our eternal rest and life with Christ. That is righteousness by faith, not works.

The Secret Rapture

The secret rapture became enormously popular after the release of the *Left Behind* series. Most of mainstream Christianity seems to believe in the secret rapture. But where does this fascinating theory come from, and is it biblical?

From Genesis to Revelation, the Bible is filled with texts and prophecies concerning the second coming of Christ and the end of time. There are more than sixty such passages in the New Testament alone. It is clear from Scripture that Jesus' second coming will be anything but secret, but there are a couple of texts that raise some questions. In the parallel chapters of Matthew 24 and Luke 17 Jesus is teaching the disciples about the end of the world. Let's break this section of Scripture down in context so we can better understand its interpretation.

Then He said to the disciples, "The days will come when you will desire to see one of the days of the Son of Man, and you will not see *it*. And they will say to you, 'Look here!' or 'Look there!' Do not go after *them* or follow *them*. For as the lightning that flashes out of one *part* under heaven shines to the other *part* under heaven, so also the Son of Man will be in His day. But first He must suffer many things and be rejected by this generation. And as it was in the days of Noah, so it will be also in the days of the Son of Man: They ate, they drank, they married wives, they were given in marriage, until the day that Noah entered the ark, and the flood came and destroyed them all. Likewise as it was also in the days of Lot: They ate, they drank, they bought, they sold, they planted, they built; but on the day that Lot went out of Sodom it rained fire and brimstone from heaven and destroyed *them* all. Even so will it be in the day when the Son of Man is revealed.

"In that day, he who is on the housetop, and his goods *are* in the house, let him not come down to take them away. And likewise the one who is in the field, let him not turn back. Remember Lot's wife. Whoever seeks to save his life will lose it, and whoever loses his life will preserve it. I tell you, in that night there will be two *men* in one bed: the one will be taken and the other will be left. Two *women* will be grinding together: the one will be taken and the other left. Two *men* will be in the field: the one will be taken and the other left."

And they answered and said to Him, "Where, Lord?" So He said to them, "Wherever the body is, there the eagles will be gathered together." (Luke 17:22–37, NKJV)

At the beginning of this text, Jesus tells His disciples to not believe anyone who says Christ is here or there because His coming will not be a secret, it will be as lightning flashes from east to west. It will be a global event, and no one will question what is happening. So if someone says to go here or there to see Christ, know that it is a false christ, even if that individual who claims to be Christ can work miracles, because Paul tells us in 2 Thessalonians 2:9 that Satan will use counterfeit powers and signs and miracles to deceive people into serving him. Jesus then goes on to compare the end of time with the time of Noah and Lot, stating that many people will go about their day like business as usual. As in those days, the people were not prepared because they ignored the teachings of Noah and Lot, and because of their unpreparedness, the flood and the fire and brimstone took them by surprise.

Jesus then says there will be a time when His people will have to flee for their safety. At the moment of realization that we must flee, Jesus says to not turn back to get anything. He says to immediately stop what we are doing and flee. Lot's wife was most likely sad about leaving her sentimental and expensive possessions and comforts behind in Sodom and Gomorrah; she clung to her life there and longed for the comforts of home so much so that she disobeyed the angels order and looked back even though she was told not to, resulting in her death.

Verses 34 and 35 are the two verses people quote in support of the secret rapture. They state that one person will be doing something with another individual and one of them will be taken and the other left. But this doesn't mean what most say it means. In verse 37, the disciples ask Jesus where these people who were taken were going, and Jesus replies, "Where there is a dead body, there the vultures will gather" (NIV). From this text alone we can see that being taken is not what we want, unlike what the popular *Left Behind* series teaches, because those who are taken end up being destroyed. Also, looking at this section as a whole, we read that Jesus is comparing the end time to the days of Noah, and it was the ones who were taken away by the flood that perished. These verses are not talking about secrecy per se, but about unexpectedness, and this unexpectedness is what He means when He says He will come as a thief. He will only come as a thief for those people who haven't sought to understand Him and His teachings about the signs of His coming, which are written in the Bible.

There is no truth in the secret rapture. The Bible is repeatedly teaching us that Jesus is coming with great power and authority and that every eye shall see Him (Luke 21:27; Rev. 1:7; 1 Thess. 4:16, 17; 2 Peter 3:10; 1 Cor. 15:52). There will be nothing secret about Jesus' coming, but there unfortunately will be many who are not expecting it.

Many believe that the time prophecies of Daniel will happen in the future right before Jesus comes, but when you read the following chapter you will learn the most logical interpretation of these time prophecies. The secret rapture is believed to take place right before or during a seven-year period of tribulation (confusingly taken from Daniel 9:24–27, but this prophecy has already been fulfilled, read the next chapter). It is hypothesized that God's people will be taken to heaven during the reign of the antichrist and the seven last plagues (there is debate as to exactly when the rapture will take place during the seven years). God will then choose 144,000 Jews to take the gospel to the whole world. They believe that there will then be a literal Armageddon war involving Israel, but that the battle will be halted by Christ's second return with His people. Israel will then accept Christ as the Messiah and enter into another covenant with Christ and reign with Him for 1,000 years. At the end of the 1,000 years, the new believers will gain immortality, and eternity will then begin.

There is a vast amount of false doctrine to these theoretical series of events. The Bible mentions nothing about Jesus' second coming being in two stages, and it is clear that those who have the seal of God will be on earth through the tribulation (see Matt. 24:21, 22) and the seven last plagues, but the Bible teaches that they will be unaffected by the plagues because they have been sealed by God, not because they are in heaven with Jesus. The Bible teaches that everyone who is dead in Christ and alive in Christ when He returns will ascend to heaven together. There is not a staggered returning. Most importantly, it is dangerously false to teach that there will be a second chance given for those who have chosen to not accept Christ. The following texts make this fairly clear:

He who is unjust, let him be unjust still; he who is filthy, let him be filthy still; he who is righteous, let him be righteous still; he who is holy, let him be holy still. And behold, I am coming quickly, and My reward *is* with Me, to give to every one according to his work. (Rev. 22:11, 12, NKJV)

As God's co-workers we urge you not to receive God's grace in vain. For he says, "In the time of my favor I heard you, and in the day of salvation I helped you." I tell you, now is the time of God's favor, now is the day of salvation. (2 Cor. 6:1, 2, NIV)

It is very clear from Revelation 22:11, 12 that once people have been sealed for God or marked for Satan there will be no second chance.

Certain theologians claim that the Greek words *parousia* and *apokalupsis* are used in the New Testament and describe two separate ways in which Jesus will return. *Parousia* means secret coming and *apokalupsis*, used in Revelation, means visible coming. Matthew 24 uses the word *parousia*, and Luke 17 uses the word *apokalupsis*, but these are parallel chapters describing the same story and events. These two words are interchangeable and prove nothing of a secret rapture.

At some unknown time in the future, seemingly soon according to Bible prophecy and the words of Jesus, there will be a latter rain or outpouring of the Holy Spirit as it was on the day of Pentecost for the disciples. This outpouring of the Holy Spirit will fall upon those who know Jesus Christ and love His law of love and who know and represent the true character of God. These individuals in the end of time follow the Lamb wherever He goes, and they will take the gospel to the entire world. They will be like the twelve disciples in the apostolic church who took the gospel to the ancient world. These people are the 144,000 (not a coincidence, 144,000 is twelve multiplied by twelve). They are the end-time disciples who will have the job of dispelling the awful accusations of Satan and revealing the true personality of God.

Many who have not known the true awesomeness of God will hear the teachings of these people, who speak with the power of the Holy Spirit, and consequently numerous people will become followers of the true God. But during this time Satan will be working to deceive like no other time. There will be false christs who perform miraculous signs and wonders, healing the sick and more. Those who don't know the truth will follow these false christs and be deceived. There will be crazy strife in the world during this time as the world goes through what Paul described as labor pains from our lack of caring of how we treat God's creation and the earth as a whole. We will begin to reap what we have sown on this earth—we have already begun to see this with many of the natural disasters that can be linked to the pollution of the air, earth, and sea. People will cry out for peace and safety from all the devastation, and those who are the mavericks, the one's who do not conform to what the world says is OK, but only follow Jesus' example, will be blamed for the strife and upheaval. These elect will refuse to follow the teachings of counterfeit peace coming from the lips of the antichrist and his disguised angels because his path to supposed peace is paved with teachings contrary to the true character of God and His commandments.

God will place a seal on those who are just, and a mark will be placed on those who love lies and guile and darkness. This is when Jesus will stand up and declare that every case has been decided: "He that is unjust, let him be unjust still: and he which is filthy, let him be filthy still: and he that is righteous, let him be righteous still: and he that is holy, let him be holy still" (Rev. 22:11, KJV). The seven plagues are soon to follow, with the seventh plague marking the end. From the throne of heaven, Jesus will say, "It is done." The realm of God will come closer and closer to the earth until the sky breaks open as Jesus returns with innumerable angels.

Those who are alive and have the mark of the beast when Jesus returns will cry for the rocks and mountains to fall on them and hide them from the Lamb who sits on the throne. The dead who are in Christ will arise from the grave with elegant, regal, and immortal bodies, and then those who are alive in Christ will be changed in the twinkling of an eye, and together we will be caught up in the air to meet Jesus and His angels.

In Revelation 20 we are told we will be in heaven for 1,000 years where we will sit on thrones and judge the unrighteous while Satan is bound here on the desolate earth. With no one to tempt, it will be as if he is in solitary confinement. There will be many questions about why some made it who we thought wouldn't and why others didn't make it who we thought would, and during this time of judging, all those questions will be answered. In the end everyone will see the true mercy, grace, and fairness of God; they will acknowledge that Jesus gave ample urging and opportunities to know the truth.

Revelation 20:7–9 tells us that there will be a second death, which means there must also be a second resurrection. All of the righteous will have already been resurrected in the first resurrection, so this second resurrection will be the wicked who have lived throughout earth's history. They will be deceived once more by Satan, who will lead them to surround the New Jerusalem in one last effort to take the city and ultimately take the power from Jesus. The unrighteous, along with Satan and his angels, will see what they gave up for their own selfishness. They could have been alive, living immortally in perfection and insurmountable joy for eternity, but they chose self over everything else.

God is a consuming fire, and in His perfect presence the wicked will be consumed. Satan, the angels, and each person will be repaid according to their works. For some the evil and darkness in their lives is so dense that it will take longer than others to be consumed by the purity of God's presence. Satan, the father of lies, will be last to be fully consumed by the fire of God. Once every trace of sin is gone, sin and those who loved it will be no more forever. The whole earth will be purified with fire, and we will get to watch Jesus recreate the new earth.

"But as it is written, Eye hath not seen, nor ear heard, neither have entered into the heart of man, the things which God hath prepared for them that love him" (1 Cor. 2:9, KJV). My heart overwhelms me with absolute joy at the thought of witnessing Jesus recreate the new earth—it is beyond awesomeness! To spend eternity by my Savior's side moves me beyond words. Today is the day of salvation, why waste our time being a slave when we can experience in our hearts and minds the joy and peace of the kingdom of heaven. "As surely as I live, says the Sovereign Lord, I take no pleasure in the death of wicked people. I only want them to turn from their wicked ways so they can live. Turn! Turn from your wickedness, O people of Israel! Why should you die?" (Ezek. 33:11, NLT; see also Joel 2:23; Acts 2; Rev. 12:17; 2 Thess. 2:9; Rev. 7; 1 Thess. 5:3; Rev. 13; Rev. 14:4; Rev. 16; Matt. 24:22; Rev. 6:16; 1 Thess. 4:16; Rev. 20; Rom. 2:6).

My preceding words are a very concise regurgitation of what the Bible teaches concerning prophecy, but wholly based on the Bible nonetheless. The rapture theory of prophetic interpretation is full of conjecture and takes a few Bible texts out of context and contradicts what much of the Bible teaches. Simply by reading the Bible and earnestly seeking truth, God will give to us discernment to see deceptions for what they are. Are we lovers of truth or lovers of lies that sooth our own egos and consciences? "But as for me and my household, we will serve the Lord" (Josh. 24:15, NIV). Sola Scriptura—the Bible only.

Eastern Philosophies and Mysticism

Many of the deceptions from these philosophies are remnants of the lie Satan told in the Garden of Eden to Eve. Debate over the mind, body, soul connection in relation to the immortality of the soul and the seeking of enlightenment has been a hot topic since the dawn of sin when Satan said, "Ye shall not surely die: For God doth know that in the day ye eat thereof, then

Meditation and prayer have become muddled. Many don't think of the two as being distinct from one another, but they are very different.

your eyes shall be opened, and ye shall be as gods" (Gen. 3:4, 5, KJV).

We find little nuggets of teachings from Eastern philosophies being taught in even the most conservative circles of Christianity today. Meditation and prayer have become muddled. Many don't think of the two as being distinct from one another, but they are very different. The meditation that eastern philosophies teach is based on the emptying of the mind. The goal is to separate mind from body in order to reach a higher state of existence.

Prayer is simply a conversation with God. No emptying of the mind, chanting, evoking of a feeling, forced mental imagery, or word repetition is necessary. God hears you from where you are. We are invited to talk to Him as we would a friend, and we are told we are invited to "come boldly unto the throne of grace, that we may obtain mercy, and find grace to help in time of need" (Heb. 4:16, KJV). I would say that prayer is completely opposite of eastern meditation because there is absolutely no emptying of the mind—all our thoughts and worries and thanks are to be shared with God.

The titles God, Christ, and Holy Spirit appear to be ambiguous in our current time. Many religions claim they are praying or thanking God, but sometimes it's not the God of the Bible—the God of Abraham, Isaac, and Jacob—they are addressing.

Some faiths such as Hinduism teach that everything is God, and God is everything. These people do not believe in a personal God, and they do not believe He is distinct from the universe, but that He is indistinguishable from it. This is called pantheism. But the one true God is a personal God, and He is separate and distinct from what He created. God is omnipresent—He is everywhere—but He is not in everything (see Luke 22:70).

A more subtle approach to pantheism is panentheism. Kabbala and Hasidic Judaism appear to teach panentheism. It is the belief the universe is within God, and God is within the universe.

The thoughts of reincarnation (karma is a part of this philosophy), animism (belief that inanimate objects have a soul or spirit), nirvana, tranquil abiding (advanced stages of concentration), meditation through emptying of the mind, the goal to supersede the rational mind and look inside ourselves to reach enlightenment, the separation of body, spirit and soul, and yin and yang (there is no good and evil, just opposite complementary forces), all have become a part of pop culture to varying degrees. Many movies include these philosophies. *Peter Pan* for instance includes animism. (Peter plays with his shadow off and on in the storyline.) Many of these teachings are very subtly included in media and some not so subtly. Remember to guard your hearts and minds that you don't take these subtle deceptions in as fact.

We all have a plethora of teachings we need to unlearn. Remember that Satan seeks to deceive as many as he can: "For we wrestle not against flesh and blood, but against principalities, against powers, against the rulers of the darkness of this world, against spiritual wickedness in high places" (Eph. 6:12, KJV).

The truth will set you free.

Chapter 6

Faith Like a Child—A Not-So-Minor Miracle

As a child I tapped into a faith in God I now long for but struggle to reclaim. Even as a teenager, up into my early twenties, I seemed to soar with confidence in God, but somehow it fizzled, ever so slowly, into almost nothingness. In the last four years I've sought that person I used to be. Amazed at the strength of my former self, God has been restoring me and my faith, but I guess that person I was will always partly be just somebody I used to know. Amazingly, although I outright rejected God at times and defied Him, God never abandoned me or let me go.

I have ridden about two or three waves of rebellion against God in my lifetime so far. In the midst of my second time of rebellion, I experienced a miracle. I was still fairly young, maybe about eighteen years old, so ironically, even in the midst of this rejection of God, I paradoxically had an enormous amount of faith in Him.

I was working my way through college as a waitress during this time. I had been saving my tip money for a couple of weeks and had not had time to go to the bank to deposit it. So when I decided to go to the mall with Nicole, I brought my stack of cash in my purse, which is a recipe for disaster.

Nicole and I found several adorable outfits we wanted to try on, and we proceeded to hold our own fashion show in the Macy's fitting room. We had a great time, but about a half hour after leaving the dressing room, I noticed I did not have my purse with me. Of course, I immediately freaked out, knowing it held hundreds of dollars.

Nicole and I retraced our steps through the store and back to the dressing rooms. The only one occupied was the one I had been in thirty minutes prior. We knocked on the door and asked the young lady in there if she had seen a purse. She got really defensive and cranky and told us no. Of course, this made her seem guilty because of her attitude. Nicole was about to kick down the door and show her a thing or two, but we calmed down and left the fitting room area. After looking everywhere, I finally told my atheist friend I was going to pray because I knew God would not let me lose all that hard earned money. She laughed at me and thought I was silly for even suggesting such an idea, but I immediately closed my eyes in the middle of Macy's and prayed out loud that God would help me find my purse and that all the money would be inside of it. I said amen, opened my eyes, and turned around, and right there on a shelf behind me was my purse. I opened it and counted the money. Every dollar was still inside. Nicole and I had looked on that shelf several times, but we had not seen it. It wasn't hard to miss either; it was brightly colored and did not blend in with the surroundings.

I began jumping up and down with excitement. I was so thankful to God. My atheist friend just stood there in awe, knowing it was truly a miracle. I often wonder if she remembers that moment and if she still remains an atheist, for we lost touch many years ago. I know it impacted my heart and mind. Even though I was running from God during that time, He never let me down. Whenever I called upon Him, He was there for me. How I could ever reject the only loyal friend a person could ever have is beyond my understanding. I love Him and am humbled every day at His grace for me.

We are never abandoned. He will never leave us nor forsake us.

We Are Not Abandoned

William Tyndale and millions of others died so you and I could own and read the words written in the Bible. These martyrs loved and sought the truth until they took their last breath.

The Bible remains the best selling book of all time. Its words are alive. It supernaturally speaks to the soul and changes lives, minds, and hearts. It gives hope, and it shapes and transforms us. It has changed history and culture. The truths written in the Bible have convicted many people's hearts so deeply that they were willing to die lest they go against its words of hope.

After the discovery of the Dead Sea scrolls, it was found that the original information of the Old Testament was at least 95 percent accurate when compared to the current Hebrew Bibles, with the disparities being in the punctuations, word order, and small details. That means the Bible's consistency in message has been retained for thousands of years. The Hebrew versions of the Bible we read now are almost exactly the same as was read by the prophets and men of old, which is incredible!

Through the Holy Spirit, God inspired the writers of the Bible to write down what He wanted to communicate to us. The Bible is not just a bunch of fables and fluffy stories. Fascinatingly, such characters as Sargon, an Assyrian king who was mentioned in the book of Isaiah, and Pontius Pilate, who was the Roman official who sentenced Christ to death, have been proven to have really existed thanks to archeological evidence, thus further validating the Bible's historical accuracy. This book, which has convicted the hearts of billions upon billions of people, possesses something no other book of faith possesses—accurate prophecy. About 27 percent of the Bible focuses on prophecy.

There have been several theoretical ways of interpreting Bible prophecy. Three main schools of interpretation are preterism, futurism, and historicism. Historicism was the original way of interpreting Bible prophecy. It makes the most sense and is the belief that prophecy is being fulfilled continuously since the time the books of the Bible were written.

The Bible, during the fourteenth century, began to be translated into common languages of that time, mostly because of John Wycliffe who was against the suppression of the Catholic Church. As the Bible became more accessible to the public, they read the prophecies and virtually all held the historicism interpretation, and most people concluded the identity of the antichrist. The preterism and futurism interpretations came into existence during the time of the reformation to take the focus off the papacy as the antichrist.

Two sixteenth century Jesuits, Francisco Ribera and Luis de Alcazar, thought of two interpretations, preterism and futurism, both of which when studied do not coalesce with the entirety of the Bible.

Very simply put, preterism suggests Bible prophecy was fulfilled in the past, during the pagan Roman empire before the papacy and holy Roman empire existed. And futurism, which the *Left Behind* series focuses on, basically is the belief that most of Bible prophecy will be fulfilled right before the second coming of Christ. I will let you research for yourself the timelines and interpretations of preterism and futurism. They are confusing, and they don't quite add up. Their interpretations are frankly illogical when you read Daniel and Revelation and the rest of the Bible in context. Daniel and John the Revelator obviously held the belief that the prophecies they were writing down would happen in succession from their time until the time of Jesus' return.

So let's look at the historicism way of interpreting Bible prophecy, and you judge how simple and understandable this interpretation is. It makes complete sense. All of the time prophecies of Isaiah and the other Old Testament prophets calculate to perfection the time of the first coming of Jesus, a fact that cannot be a coincidence. God gave us these prophecies as encouragement. He knew that when we saw the fulfillment of what was predicted thousands of years ago we would be encouraged in our faith, knowing that He has not abandoned us and will return again as He promised.

The key to understanding Bible prophecy is to study the Bible in its entirety and let the Bible interpret itself. The answers to Bible prophecy don't lie in some human philosophy or out of context texts; they lie in scripture as a whole. God did this on purpose, for He wants us to seek Him and lean not on our own understanding. And by seeking Him we will get to know who He truly is. We will also gain discernment and better understand the voice of the Holy Spirit, recognizing it from the whispers of Satan's deceptions.

The Bible is rich in symbolism. The study of the sanctuary and all its exacting minute details is a symbolic playing out of future events. It all pointed forward to Jesus' first coming and His gift of salvation. After His death the focus of the sanctuary shifted to what Christ is doing in the heavenly sanctuary and what He will be doing until He comes again.

In Numbers 14:34 and Ezekiel 4:6, it is said that a day equals a year in Bible prophecy. Knowing this equation, the time prophecies in Daniel add up perfectly to accurately predict the succession of kingdoms of the ancient world.

But before we go into the exacting time prophecies of Daniel, let's begin with the awesome dream that King Nebuchadnezzar had in Daniel 2. The king had a dream that he couldn't remember, but he was very troubled concerning it and threatened his astrologers and wise men with death if they couldn't tell him the dream and its interpretation. Of course, only a supernatural intervention could allow for this insight and interpretation. Daniel, one of the captured young men from Jerusalem, was given divine inspiration to not only see the dream the king dreamt, but also tell its interpretation.

In his dream King Nebuchadnezzar saw a giant statue. Daniel told the king that the statue was a timeline describing the then-current Babylonian empire and the empires that would come in succession until the second coming of Christ. Babylon was the head of gold (605–539 BC), the following inferior empire was the Medo-Persian Empire (539–331 BC), which was represented as the chest and arms of silver, the third empire was Greece (331–168 BC) as the thighs of bronze, the fourth was Rome (168 BC–AD 476) as the legs of iron, and the feet of iron mixed with clay represents the divided nations of western Europe that broke up out of the Roman Empire. The rock that crushed the statue represents the second coming of Christ and His everlasting kingdom. These are the main four ruling empires that affected the Jewish nation in our world's history since the time of Babylon.

"He has made you the ruler over all the inhabited world and has put even the wild animals and birds under your control. You are the head of gold.

But after your kingdom comes to an end, another kingdom, inferior to yours, will rise to take your place. After that kingdom has fallen, yet a third kingdom, represented by bronze, will rise to rule the world. Following that kingdom, there will be a fourth one, as strong as iron. That kingdom will smash and crush all previous empires, just as iron smashes and crushes everything it strikes. The feet and toes you saw were a combination of iron and baked clay, showing that this kingdom will be divided. Like iron mixed with clay, it will have some of the strength of iron. But while some parts of it will be as strong as iron, other parts will be as weak as clay. This mixture of iron and clay also shows that these kingdoms will try to strengthen themselves by forming alliances with each other through intermarriage. But they will not hold together, just as iron and clay do not mix.

During the reigns of those kings, the God of heaven will set up a kingdom that will never be destroyed or conquered. It will crush all these kingdoms into nothingness, and it will stand forever. That is the meaning of the rock cut from the mountain, though not by human hands, that crushed to pieces the statue of iron, bronze, clay, silver, and gold. The great God was showing the king what will happen in the future. The dream is true, and its meaning is certain" (Dan. 2:38–45, NLT).

This same timeline of empires, represented by beasts, is foretold in Daniel 7 in greater detail. The lion represented Babylon; the bear, Medo-Persia; the leopard, Greece; and the fierce beast different from all other beast, Rome. Each beast shares similar characteristics to its corresponding empire, such as the ten horns on the last beast (and also the ten toes on the feet of the statue), which represented the divided kingdoms of Europe after the fall of the Roman Empire, including the Huns or Alamanni (Germany), Ostrogoths (wiped out), Visigoths (Spain), Franks (France), Vandals (wiped out), Suevi (Portugal), Burgundians (Switzerland), Heruli (wiped out), Saxons (England), and Lombards (Italy).

"These four huge beasts represent four kingdoms that will arise from the earth. But in the end, the holy people of the Most High will be given the kingdom, and they will rule forever and ever" (Dan. 7:17, 18, NLT).

Daniel gets more and more detailed, using different animal symbols for each of these empires as you read through the book. For instance, two empires of the four are outright listed: "The ram which thou sawest having two horns are the kings of Media and Persia. And the rough goat is the king of Grecia: and the great horn that is between his eyes is the first king" (Dan. 8:20, 21, KJV).

It is also interesting to note that the beast in Revelation 13 is a combination of the beasts of Daniel 7, but John listed the parts of the beast in opposite order as Daniel because he was standing in the prophetic future looking back to the time of Daniel.

This book could be hundreds of pages long if we delved into prophecy. I've barely touched on the subject. I'm just highlighting basic aspects to peak your interest. I hope you will study the Bible for yourself and learn these amazing truths. They are not scary, and they don't mean gloom and doom as many hellfire and brimstone preachers teach. In fact, the book of Revelation has a blessing attached to it for those who read and study it: "Blessed is the one who reads aloud the words of this prophecy, and blessed are those who hear it and take to heart what is written in it, because the time is near" (Rev. 1:3, NIV). The prophecies of the Bible are just teachings wrapped in symbolism to show us what the future holds. We are to study and understand so we will not be deceived.

As we close this chapter, I want to look at one more time prophecy. This will blow you away if your mind hasn't already been blown. "And he said unto me, Unto two thousand and three hundred days; then shall the sanctuary be cleansed" (Dan. 8:14, KJV).

One of the main Bible time prophecies is the 2300 days mentioned above. In Daniel 9 Gabriel comes to further interpret the 2300-day prophecy and begins to incorporate other time prophecies which are within the 2300-day prophecy.

"O Daniel, I have now come forth to give you skill to understand. At the beginning of your supplications the command went out, and I have come to tell *you*, for you *are* greatly beloved; therefore consider the matter, and understand the vision:

"Seventy weeks are determined
For your people and for your holy city,
To finish the transgression,
To make an end of sins,
To make reconciliation for iniquity,
To bring in everlasting righteousness,
To seal up vision and prophecy,
And to anoint the Most Holy.
"Know therefore and understand,
That from the going forth of the command
To restore and build Jerusalem
Until Messiah the Prince,
There shall be seven weeks and sixty-two weeks;
The street shall be built again, and the wall,
Even in troublesome times.
"And after the sixty-two weeks
Messiah shall be cut off, but not for Himself;

And the people of the prince who is to come
Shall destroy the city and the sanctuary.
The end of it *shall be* with a flood,
And till the end of the war desolations are determined.
Then he shall confirm a covenant with many for one week;
But in the middle of the week
He shall bring an end to sacrifice and offering.
And on the wing of abominations shall be one who makes desolate,
Even until the consummation, which is determined,
Is poured out on the desolate." (Dan. 9:22–27, NKJV)

If a day is a year, then the 70 weeks mentioned above equals 490 years. This prophecy is part of the 2300-day prophecy in the preceding chapter. Gabriel tells Daniel the going forth command to rebuild Jerusalem will mark the beginning of these prophecies. This decree was in 457 BC. The 490 years was given to the Jews to spread the good news about God to the world. Within those 490 years, there would be 69 weeks until the Messiah our Prince would come. Sixty-nine weeks equals 483 years till the time of Christ. So 457 BC plus 483 years brings us to AD 27, which was when Jesus was baptized and began His ministry.

Gabriel goes on to say that He would confirm His covenant for one week, or seven years, but in the midst of the week He would be sacrificed. This, too, all adds up. Three and a half years after Jesus began His ministry He was crucified in AD 31. After Jesus' death, for three and a half years, the remainder of the prophecy, the gospel was preached to the Jews by Jesus' disciples. At the end of the second three and half years, Stephen was stoned in AD 34. His vision of the history of the Jewish nation was the conclusion of the gospel to be preached solely to the Jews because of their conscious rejection of the Messiah and His prophets who came before Him. Now the gospel was to be preached among the Gentiles.

After the 490 years, 1810 years remained in the prophecy until the cleansing of the sanctuary, bringing us to 1844. As some of you might remember from history class, in 1844 there was something called the Great Disappointment. A man named William Miller was sure from studying Bible prophecy that

1844, the close of the 2300-day prophecy, was the year Jesus would return, specifically in the fall of 1844. But of course Jesus didn't come.

Notice that Gabriel told Daniel the sanctuary would be cleansed in 1844, not that Jesus would return. The subject of the cleansing of the sanctuary is a rather complex topic that deserves its own book. I will let you research the significance of what happened in the sanctuary in 1844. Hint: the sanctuary we are talking about is not an earthly sanctuary. "For Christ did not enter a sanctuary made with human hands that was only a copy of the true one; he entered heaven itself, now to appear for us in God's presence" (Heb. 9:24, NIV).

The other significant time prophecy is mentioned in Daniel 7:25; 12:7 and Revelation 11:2, 3; 12:14, 6; 13:5. In these texts, the Bible mentions a timeframe lasting for "a time, times and half a time," which is the same time period as the 1260 days and the 42 months. An important note here to remember with this prophecy is that the years in the Bible were lunar years and had 360 days, which is also why we have 360 degrees on our compass. The 1260 years began with Emperor Justinian's decree in AD 538 to destroy the Ostrogoths because they did not believe in the Trinity. Thus began the reign of papal supremacy. It reigned for exactly 1260 years until February 10, 1798, when General Berthier, under Napoleon's leadership, marched into Rome and renounced the pope's temporal authority. This is when the papacy received its deadly wound as mentioned in Revelation 13:3. As of 1844 every Bible time prophecy has been fulfilled. We are living in the very last days of earth's history. According to Daniel's statue timeline, the very next event to occur is the coming of Jesus Christ.

Below is a chart that is a visual aid of all the time prophecies of Daniel and Revelation. It can be easier to understand when outlined in a visual way.

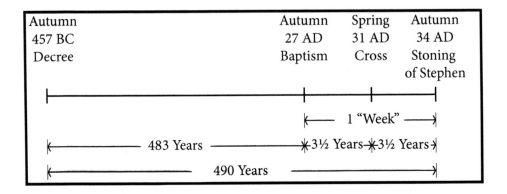

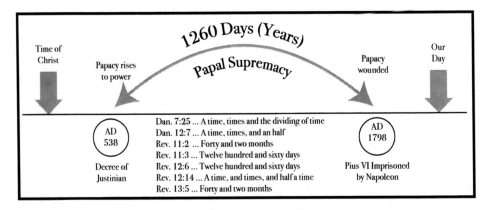

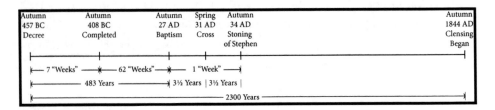

I have barely touched on prophecy, but I wanted to whet your appetite for Bible prophecy and how it fits into our past, present, and future. It's amazing when you take the time to study it in context with the rest of the Bible. We should not be afraid of it. God has not abandoned us. He will help us understand what we study in preparation for the return of the King of kings.

Chapter 7

Finishing the Race

"Our greatest fear should not be of failure but of succeeding at things in life that don't really matter," wrote Francis Chan, an American pastor from California.

So much of our lives is wasted on just trying to survive. We are alive, but we are not really living. Why should we continue to just barely survive when the ability to thrive is within our reach? That is what God offers us. He came that we might have life and experience it more abundantly. In knowing Him we can find our true selves, which means we can find what makes us truly happy, instead of seeking and never finding.

> *We are alive, but we are not really living. Why should we continue to just barely survive when the ability to thrive is within our reach?*

Most of us secretly or not so secretly wish we could hop into a time machine and travel back in time for a do-over. Mistakes and regrets crush us, but Jesus offers us a new beginning. He heals diseases caused by our own damaging choices; He opens up new doors to life and gives hope and peace and new possibilities. God is the inventor of second chances. We can experience the peace and freedom of heaven, a foretaste of eternity, on this earth if we live our life for Jesus. I view the Comforter, the Holy Spirit, as a down payment and promise of eternal life. Why should we let Satan and his chains hold us back? I dare you to run this race with Jesus. He promises to give "power to the weak and strength to the powerless. Even youths will become weak and tired, and young men will fall in exhaustion. But those who trust in the Lord will find new strength. They will soar high on wings like eagles. They will run and not grow weary. They will walk and not faint" (Isa. 40:29–31, NLT).

Throughout our lives we may find ourselves falling in and out of various categories pertaining to our relationship or lack of relationship with God. Below I mention a few of those categories in which I've moved in and out of a few times myself, and each time I've come out with a new takeaway lesson. So here's some food for thought.

If you don't believe in the Creator, and you are somehow reading this book, I beg of you to test what I have written about God. If you look for Him, you will find Him because He is always beside you. He is pursuant, but He is also a gentleman. He will not force His way in.

I lived a life apart from God and sought out other philosophies and faiths, but they never sought me back. Only when I searched for God did I find the truth. All other philosophies and faiths lead down an empty, answerless road, but God is real. He has emotions, thoughts, and feelings that can be hurt. He is a personal God who is love and who, just like us, desires relationships. We, after all, are His creation, His children. We instinctively know we exist for something more than ourselves.

If I could choose one text to sum up my book, it would be Habakkuk 2:4, "Look at the proud person. He is not right in himself. But the righteous person will live because of his faithfulness" (GW).

I believe that when the text says "because of his faithfulness" it is talking about Christ's faithfulness to us, the very theme I've been repeating over and over in this book. If we look to ourselves, if we trust in our own merits and try to be righteous by our own actions, we are being proud and self-centered. We cannot be right in and of ourselves or on our own accord as the text above says, but the righteous will be those who focus on Jesus' faithfulness and pardoning love, which is our strength and hope.

So, as you fight this good fight and round the corner to the last .2 miles of this marathon, don't let the things that drag you down have power over your life. There is only true freedom and joy in knowing Jesus. Remember His words, "Be strong and courageous. Do not be afraid or terrified because of them, for the Lord your God goes with you; he will never leave you nor forsake you" (Deut. 31:6, NIV). To know I'm never truly alone and that who I am is infinitely valuable to the one and only all-powerful God is the greatest comfort I can know. He would rather have had died an eternal death than live an eternal life without me, and He remains forever divinely tied to our lowly humanity—a divinely beautiful truth that we are incapable of fully understanding but for eternity will attempt to comprehend.

Christ is our righteousness; Christ is our faithfulness; because He is love.

[God] gave [Jesus] to the fallen race. To assure us of His immutable counsel of peace, God gave His only-begotten Son to become one of the human family, forever to retain His human nature. This is the pledge that God will fulfill His word. "Unto us a child is born, unto us a son is given: and the government shall be upon His shoulder." God has adopted human nature in the person of His Son, and has carried the same into the highest heaven. It is the "Son of man" who shares the throne of the universe. It is the "Son of man" whose name shall be called, "Wonderful, Counselor, The mighty God, The everlasting Father, The Prince of Peace." Isaiah 9:6. The I AM is the Daysman between God and humanity, laying His hand upon both. He who is "holy, harmless, undefiled, separate from sinners," is not ashamed to call us brethren. Hebrews 7:26; 2:11. In Christ the family of earth and the family of heaven are bound together. Christ glorified is our brother. Heaven is enshrined in humanity, and humanity is enfolded in the bosom of Infinite Love. (Ellen G. White, *The Desire of Ages*, pp. 25, 26)

Pictures

Kris's homecoming from his third deployment. He had three deployments in three years, it was pretty rough, but the homecomings were beyond joyous.

This was during our infamous Cataract Canyon river trip on our lunch break right before we hit the crazy canyon waters. You can see the petrified/ trying-to-act-brave look on my face.

I traveled to Dubai twice for Kris's port calls to visit him while he was on deployment. This King Penguin is named Wally and he lives inside Ski Dubai which is in the Dubai Mall. His name is Wally because his caretakers said he would just sit and stare at the walls of his enclosure for hours. He was the sweetest thing, and so patient with all of our group, touching, petting and kissing him. His softness was beyond what I would have imagined.

This picture was taken at the elephant sanctuary in Kuala Lumpur, Malaysia, I was there visiting Kris for another port call.

Delicate Arch with the La Sal Mountains in the background. Delicate Arch is in Arches National Park near Moab, Utah. This was taken during our honeymoon trip to Moab right before we left for our rafting trip. This is one of my favorite places in the world.

A low-angle view of the top of Delicate Arch with the gorgeous blue sky contrasting with the white clouds and red sandstone. Blue serenity....

*If you take HWY 128 from Grand Junction, CO, to Moab, UT, you go through
Castle Valley in Utah. The lonely Colorado River winds through this canyon.
It is stunningly beautiful, and the smells are incredibly sweet.
If only there existed a scratch-and-sniff photo.*

*This little beauty is a Collared Lizard. He was hanging out on a rock by
Independence Monument in Grand Junction, CO. This was one
of our stops on our river rafting honeymoon trip.*

Kris and I took our Jeep rental on an off-road trail to a plateau overlooking Castle Valley in Utah.

Just hours after our tour of the elephant sanctuary in Malaysia, Kris and I were married in Kuala Lumpur by the chaplain of his carrier, the John C. Stennis. Kris was barely home in three years because of all his deployments. It worked out to be easier and more timely, to fly me out to meet him to be married while in port, plus it was very romantic. An epic day I will never forget.

References

Bailey, David H. "How Reliable Are Geologic Dates?" Q&A: Evolution, Creationism and Intelligent Design. *http://1ref.us/7s* (accessed November 13, 2014).

Browne, Malcolm W. "Errors Are Feared in Carbon Dating." *The New York Times. http://1ref.us/7r* (accessed November 12, 2014).

Chapman, Glen W. "The Problems With Carbon Dating." Chapman Research Group. *http://1ref.us/7t* (accessed June 17, 2013).

Gibson, Ty. *A God Named Desire.* Nampa, ID: Pacific Press Publishing Association, 2010.

Lucado, Max. *Six Hours One Friday.* Sisters, OR: Multnomah Publishers Inc, 1989.

Luskin, Casey. "What Are the Top Ten Problems With Darwinian Evolution?" Evolution News and Views. *http://1ref.us/7n* (accessed March 24, 2014).

Moran, Laurence. "Evolution is a Fact and a Theory." The TalkOrigins Archive. *http://1ref.us/7m* (accessed April 7, 2014).

Omartian, Stormie. *The Power of a Praying Wife Devotional.* Eugene, OR: Harvest House Publishers, Eugene, 2011.

Theobald, Douglas. "The Scientific Case for Common Descent." 29+ Evidences for Macroevolution. *http://1ref.us/7o* (accessed April 16, 2014).

"The Top 30 Problems With the Big Bang." Meta Research. *http://1ref.us/7q* (accessed April 17, 2014).

Venden, Morris L. *95 Thesis on Righteousness by Faith.* Nampa, ID: Pacific Press Publishing Association, 1997.

White, Ellen G. *The Desire of Age.* Mountain View, CA: Pacific Press Publishing Association, 1898.

Wilkins, John. "Spontaneous Generation and the Origin of Life." The TalkOrigins Archive. *http://1ref.us/7p* (accessed April 16, 2014).

We invite you to view the complete
selection of titles we publish at:

www.TEACHServices.com

scan with your mobile
device to go directly
to our website

Please write or email us your praises, reactions, or
thoughts about this or any other book we publish at:

www.TEACHServices.com ◆ **(800) 367-1844**

P.O. Box 954
Ringgold, GA 30736

Info@TEACHServices.com

TEACH Services, Inc., titles may be purchased in bulk for
educational, business, fund-raising, or sales promotional use.
For information, please e-mail:

BulkSales@TEACHServices.com

Finally if you are interested in seeing
your own book in print, please contact us at

publishing@TEACHServices.com

We would be happy to review your manuscript for free.

CPSIA information can be obtained at www.ICGtesting.com
Printed in the USA
LVOW10s2125220615

443421LV00018B/71/P